Praise for **Body as Sar**

"Roberta Pughe's *Body As Sanctuary for Soul* is a tour de force for our time. Pughe weaves the practices of psyche and the sacred together in an embodied way. She diagnoses our cultural malaise and how this is reflected in much psychotherapy today. Like Meister Eckhart, she paints a vision of the tiny seed buried within the soul, that once nourished with our invocation, we become alert to it, and as implicit memory of it unfolds, we grow in explicit clarity of our life's Dream; we reconfigure our lives to support its embodied manifestation. Not only does she tell us about the seed and potential of our soul, she shows us how to live it, do it, be it. Readers will find in these pages teachings and practical methods for unveiling and actualizing of their deepest longings. Psychotherapists and shamanic practitioners will find *Body As Sanctuary for Soul* rich in insights into the intricacies of a soul-filled life, the healing of soul injury, and much more. I give it four stars."

–C. Michael Smith, Ph.D., clinical psychologist and international
shamanic teacher, and author of *Jung and Shamanism in Dialogue*
and *Psychotherapy and the Sacred*

"In this era of uncertainty, many people are desperately looking for guidance and direction. In this remarkable book, Roberta Pughe tells her readers that there is no better teacher than their own soul. This is an important message, one that will encourage people to seek wisdom from the deepest parts of themselves rather than from outside sources that could easily lead them into cults, extremist groups, and authoritarian movements. Drawing from shamanism, Yoga, and ancient traditions, *Body As Sanctuary for Soul* delivers a message that is upbeat, positive, and life-affirming."

–Stanley Krippner, PhD., Alan Watts Professor of Psychology, Saybrook
University, Co-author *Personal Mythology* and *Extraordinary Dreams*

"What is so refreshing about *Body As Sanctuary for Soul* is Roberta Pughe's intelligent observations from cultures around the world of some very simple spiritual principles that many of today's seekers miss — we have everything within to heal and transform our limited experience of life and it begins with an "unlearning" of things we were taught by well-meaning teachers, and connecting deep within ourselves and with the community of souls we have gathered around our lives. This is a book I will refer back to often."

—Peter Sterios, yoga teacher, architect, and founder
of eco-yoga products company MANDUKA

"In her powerful new book Roberta Pughe at long last unites the traditions of Shamanism, Gestalt therapy, Jungian psychology, Yoga, Buddhism, and Christian Mysticism as a means to develop ones true relationship with their soul. In doing so she makes a valuable contribution to the fields of psychotherapy and spiritual practice. *Body As Sanctuary for Soul* is a rich book that, rather than rushing through, you might want to linger and chew on to get the extraordinary flavors."

—Jose Luis Stevens Ph.D., author of *Awaken the Inner Shaman*,
The Power Path, and *Transforming Your Dragons*

"With great expertise and intimacy, Roberta Pughe guides us through a deep and rich exploration of the inner landscapes where body and soul join. Synthesizing practices of shamanism, psychotherapy and wisdom traditions, *Body As Sanctuary for Soul* orients us to the essential and meaningful path of becoming a true and whole human being guided by soul. A wise and profound call to living the fullness of life!"

—Felicia Norton and Charles Smith, senior meditation teachers in the
Sufi tradition and authors of *An Emerald Earth: Cultivating a
Natural Spirituality* and *Serving Creative Beauty in our World*

"How welcome to find a book that awakens our awareness to the deep and universal yearning to feel connected with our Soul's source. The Soul is by nature illusive, but in *Body As Sanctuary for Soul*, Roberta Pughe gives help and comfort to many who suffer from a sense of separation in our turbulent and hyperlinked lives. She opens doors to the way in which mystics, shamans, artists, yogis, and people who live authentic lives in touch with the rhythms of nature have found to transform pain into love and return home to the essence of Soul."

—Angela Farmer, international inspiration for teachers and students of yoga

Body as Sanctuary for Soul

An Embodied Enlightenment Practice

ROBERTA PUGHE

White Cloud Press
Ashland, Oregon

White Cloud Press books may be purchased for educational, business, or sales promotional use. For information, please write:

Special Market Department
White Cloud Press
PO Box 3400
Ashland, OR 97520
Website: www.whitecloudpress.com

Cover art © 2015 by Sigi Dawn Lostimolo. Use with permission.
Cover and interior design by Christy Collins, C Book Services
Interior illustrations by David Ruppe, Impact Publications

Printed in South Korea.
First edition: 2015
15 16 17 18 19 20   10 9 8 7 6 5 4 3 2 1

Library of Congress Cataloging-in-Publication Data

Pughe, Roberta Mary.
  Body as sanctuary for soul : an embodied enlightenment practice / Roberta M. Pughe, LMFT.
       pages cm
    Includes bibliographical references and index.
   ISBN 978-1-935952-46-6 (paperback)
  1. Mind and body. 2. Plato. 3. Gestalt psychology. I. Title.
  BF151.P84 2015
  158--dc23
                              2015009070

I dedicate this book to Zach and Josh
Your endless love and enduring support inspire my inquiries

CONTENTS

PREFACE
The Inseparable Body and Soul

Without the soul the body is dead and without the body the soul is unreal.

C. G. JUNG

Thus Yahweh says to Moses: "And let them make me a sanctuary;
that I may dwell among them."

EXODUS 25:8

ANCIENT KNOWLEDGE REMEMBERED

On most nights, the midnight sky and the moon keep me awake at night. Nature's mysteries lure me out the window, but the four walls of my room function as a dam, trying to barricade me from the translucence that wants to cascade through my body. As I lie in my bed, often feeling unusually estranged from nature at this hour, I think about Pierre Teilhard de Chardin's notion that "the universe is a living host" and wonder about the interconnectedness of all things.

Even modern astrophysicists confirm our perception of ourselves as separate from nature as flawed. We all derive from the stars and are far more connected than our minds can comprehend. The universe itself exists within each one of us. You and I are actually part of the night sky. Our natures are far more connected to nature than perhaps we want to admit. Astrophysicists claim we belong to "it," but we already knew we belonged to "it" long before they ever said we did. Somewhere, buried deep inside all of us is a tiny seed of memory that knows, subjectively, that certain things are true.

This internal knowing is fueled by a tiny seed that is *a state of consciousness* unto itself, existing inside each one of us, waiting to be invoked; in fact, this tiny seed holds a latent desire to be awakened. Once alert, memory unravels and we are reconfigured in the knowledge of our true nature. Once remembered, our souls allow us to see our dream's destiny with greater clarity. We are then able to connect to our full, pure potential as this state of consciousness unveils itself for us from a constant, though typically veiled reality. This is not a state of waking, sleeping, or lucid dreaming but is something else. This is the realm of the soul and there are certain laws that govern this state of being. What seem like riddles become secrets revealed. Through a path of direct revelation, expanded states of consciousness allow the invisible to be made visible, the unseen to be seen and the unknown, known. Through a daily, disciplined spiritual practice and commitment to this discovery process as "a conscious return," the sacred mysteries of the Soul Realm can be uncovered, one pearl at a time.

Our finite bodies are the containers for our infinite souls. This physical existence—the body—is what the soul seeks to find its full expression through the physical realm. The truth is that our souls are an inextricable part of the whole of the universe—encompassing the totality of who we are and the whole of the cosmos, the Cosmic Soul—which connects us with the power of this majestic universe, introducing us to transcendence—all that is. Our individual souls, informed from the world of Cosmic Soul, are daily endeavoring to infuse our human "reality" with greater wisdom, purpose, and meaning as we return to the innocence we once enjoyed. Once we truly comprehend this "re-membering" from the inside out, we begin to understand that it is not that we *have a soul* but that we *are our soul.*

When self-perception comprehends ourselves to *be* Soul and not merely to intermittently *access* soul (as a compartmentalized aspect of who we are), we then live as a unified whole with our core essence. The truth of who we are designed to be rises to the surface. We begin to understand that the Cosmic Soul, the eyes of truth, is always watching to ensure our soul's unfolding toward complete incarnate fulfillment. Whether we understand or we don't, whether we believe or we doubt, our soul eventually ensures its destiny—it's just a matter of time (or lifetimes). Because our soul is the center pin of our existence, not just an aspect of who we are as a body/mind, certain things must simply occur—as in life's purpose—and will come to pass without our invitation, so that our soul can ascend in its designed, evolutionary manner. When our lives are viewed conceptually as taking place in a type of sacralized cosmos (as opposed to a desacralized cosmos—a worldview without Soul), the meaning of our lives and our central dreams for our existence becomes clear. This satisfies our great hunger for meaning. We begin to understand that we do, in fact, require tools for living out this daily soul embodiment and that we may be lacking some sort of guide to find the path home. This courageous acknowledgement allows our soul to move toward fulfilling its divine purpose.

Perhaps the reason we humans seek transcendence (and have done so cross-culturally for centuries) is that we are designed, created, even hardwired to connect with something greater than ourselves. This allows us to find contentment—to belong. As Plato affirmed so many years ago, *a soul must be allowed to perform its proper function.* So, what is a soul's function? Learning how to remain tethered to our soul's knowing will potentially allow us to discern its otherworldly function. We learn that there is a pathway to comprehending and interpreting this knowledge and finding greater purpose and meaning in our lives. Even if there may have been dreams that were derailed along the way or a secret life's wish submerged by our own unaware choices, our soul offers us the power and the clarity to rebirth those dreams and drive them home to completion. The very nature of our soul's functional task can be so mind-boggling that it causes many to seek access to an altered state (which is not necessarily transcendent) through mood-altering substances.

My intent in writing this book is to teach you how to access transcendence—a state of ecstasy and bliss regardless of life's circumstances—through a "natural" expanded state of consciousness. This skill set requires the engagement of discernment—through connection with your very soul—unencumbered by any hallucinogenic herbs or psychoactive substances.

Understandably, your logical mind is going to ask lots of questions about this process while you are reading. As "rational beings," we feel vindicated by the scientific developments that provide quantifiable evidence for that which we have instinctively known to be true all along. Somewhere within our fanciful minds, we recognize that we have known the *truth* before science or any other authoritative discipline could provide the proof. The notion that we are "spiritual beings having a human experience," and not the other way around[1] may confirm our internal recognition of certain basic universal truths.

As the Harvard psychologist and philosopher William James puts it, "It is as if there were in the human consciousness a sense of reality, a perception of what we may call 'something there,' more deep and more general than any of the special and particular 'senses' by which the current psychology supposes existent realities to be originally revealed."[2]

Our soul, that aspect of us which is eternal and never dies, knows that we are timeless and that our finite bodies are merely the containers—the incarnate temples—carrying the knowledge of the infinite. This mysterious understanding from within is what Plato called "the seed of memory." This consciousness is our soul communing with the larger Cosmic Soul of the Soul Realm.

But why does any of this matter? It matters because, as we become more intimately acquainted with who we truly are, through our soul's perception, we realize that our life's purpose can unfold with greater clarity. We develop the capacity and the capability to fulfill our soul's calling, our dreams, our destiny in the daily choices we make with our lives, and collectively we work in service to fulfill the mission of the larger Cosmic Soul.

After thirty-some years practicing as a psychotherapist, listening to folks delve into the meaning of life, I have become aware of two primary issues. The first is that the field of psychology is lacking in providing a comprehensive skill set equipped to adequately heal the totality of the human being, particularly the ills of the soul. Second is the recurring observation that, despite our human fixation with obtaining gratification, people seek more than pleasure. While pleasure is a religion for some, for others, pleasure alone isn't enough. Throughout the ages, many spiritual seekers have pursued altered, expanded states of consciousness so that they could access "something more." Such efforts may be seen as merely a means of escaping the mundaneness of life's daily grind. But, in some paradoxical way, another explanation may be that instead of the sacred seeking to be integrated with the profane, it is really the profane that is seeking to be penetrated by the sacred. One interpretation to consider is that it is part of our hardwiring to understand that the sacred is equivalent not only to knowledge but, in the last analysis, to reality. Just as, to be made real, the soul needs the body, it also needs the physical realities of this earthly existence in order to come into fullness of being and be seen in its distinctive ontological nature. This primal need may be expressing an unquenchable thirst—referred to as the great hunger in many indigenous societies—for a more in-depth comprehension of human *being*.

In my practice, many of my clients have described an emptiness or lack of fulfillment in attending solely to life's daily challenges through a physical/material lens. It is in these dismal moments that we may reach for a second or third cocktail to numb out, jump online to spend more money we don't have, or seek out some activity to silence the reality of this human impasse. Often, we do not consciously recognize or admit that these lifeless moments may be due to the fact that our souls are long lost or unknown or, perhaps, fragmented off, lost and imprisoned somewhere in a distant universe. Much of our society is so cut off from a soulful perspective that many do not believe our souls are knowable, and some question whether we even have a soul—until we become consciously awakened through an experience of transcendence or, para-doxically, through deep suffering that invites a spiritual awakening as we seek to find a way to accept and embrace life's circumstances.

When the veil lifts and the threshold reveals itself as an undeniable passage we must step through, then and only then do we open ourselves to contemplating the existence of ecstatic states of consciousness and perhaps pondering the realm of Mystery, the Soul. While some may casually refer to this as "the season of my awakening," it is usually the beginning of a conscious ascension of our soul, in a process of deliberate evolution.

Our souls, which are eternal and never die, understand that we are timeless and that our finite bodies are merely containers carrying the knowledge of Infinity. This mysterious knowing within comes from the seed of memory from the Soul Realm, which must be cultivated to be actualized. Our souls know that there is a universe constantly cheering us on, where the drums never stop drumming, and that our evolution never stops spiraling upward. Our souls know this, even though science hasn't yet proved it. But how does one water this seed of memory with the proper spiritual fertilizer so that the soul-retrieval process can occur? According to different mystical traditions that teach the sacred knowledge of the mysteries, as well as cross-cultural (yet similar) oral knowledge disseminated through global practices of various spiritual traditions, there are specific guidelines that must be followed if we are to pass through the eye of the needle. Once we pass through the portal, or threshold, the veil is lifted and our soul sews our destiny's tapestry. Our inner vision sees and our feet follow, walking in step—in these bodies—as the Great Ones stitch in support of our soul's ascension, one divine stitch, one human step at a time.

My soul remembers the day—I've seen it many times—when I lived as one with my horse in the woods. I toss and turn as memory reveals itself, like a lover unraveling to me. In these moments, I am certain the Soul Realm sees me and wants me to see it. Most nights I drum myself to sleep, caressing my frame drum with the blue serpent on its skin, feeling eased by its heartbeat. My drum connects me to that primordial, peaceful state in which Infinity is extended like a movie reel for my soul's relief. In this space, time is timeless. I am certain that I know what I know. I see and then I see again, only more clearly, with each passing night. Some nights the mist is thick and I feel as though I do not see at all. On these nights, I only hope that my struggle to be faithful in my pursuit will matter. Usually, though, the secret mysteries reveal themselves ever more to me in these twilight hours, when the veil is thin and the moon talks. The midnight sky awakens the curiosity of my inner vision, whispering to me as if calling me deeper into the thicket of my soul, the woods not yet trailed.

The unknown cave within—our interior's fertile void—beckons to each one of us, confirming our soul's longing to be known and pursued.

The Cosmic Soul responds from the Soul Realm in a generous manner to those who seek, bestowing gifts of inner vision on those who believe and exhibit "eyes to see and ears to hear." These gifts are what we refer to as magick, or "seer sight," similar to the image of soul depicted in the Bible verse, "We walk by faith, not by sight" (2 Cor. 5:7). The faith spoken of here is an internal knowing in the dark. Just as a shaman is one who sees in the dark and sheds light on the dark shadows, when we learn to live integrating shamanic practices, we learn that we can see, not merely with the physical eyes in the physical plane, but through the inner landscape of the "third eye," known instinctively through the wisdom and intuitive intelligence of the soul. Most of us have had some sort of experience with our own souls, however fleeting, which will resonate with what I write about—if we let it.

I believe in you, my Soul. Loaf with me on the grass, loose the stop from your throat. Only the lull I like, the hum of your valved voice. I mind how once we lay, such a transparent summer morning, swiftly arose and spread around me the peace and knowledge that pass all the argument of the earth.

WALT WHITMAN

Back in the 1980s, I built my private practice, working with survivors of early childhood trauma. I have learned over the years to deeply respect the fact that many trauma survivors instinctively know how to cultivate communication with metaphysical realities; however buried their soul may be, lying dormant in their psyche is the knowledge that reattachment with their soul is a requirement for healing and wholeness. Many trauma survivors have learned, through dissociative, creative adaptations, to "take flight" into otherworldly realms. This magical flight into metaphysical spheres has often saved them and allowed them to survive their traumatic physical circumstances. A combination of psychotherapy and shamanic healing has helped these clients cognitively understand their souls' language, which they knew intuitively, allowing them to bring the fragmented puzzle pieces of their lives back together, until they ultimately reached wholeness, integration, and connectedness. It appears that survivors of trauma have what Dr. Donald Kalsched has called "privileged access" to the Soul Realm.[3] Trauma and suffering are often the portal of access through which we enter into a deeper understanding of magical flight with the soul, comfortably traversing otherworldly spheres. Perhaps through dissociation and depersonalization—psychological terms for trauma survivors' creative adaptations to trauma—they learned early on to trust traversing the worlds of earth and sky as a survival mechanism. Many trauma survivors, intimately familiar with magical flight, have always known as "subjective, true fact" that this physical reality is clearly not all there is.

For some, admitting to beliefs that are marginalized by mainstream society (or believing in a reality other than the one commonly accepted) may arouse fear of judgment, with ensuing skepticism and disbelief. For others, if science has not extended its stamp of approval, it may be more difficult to support an internal belief structure affirming the existence of such things as expanded states of consciousness or the Soul Realm. It is often through actual experience that we grow in affirming our own subjective truth. The science of valuing experience as sufficiently authoritative is called phenomenology. It is through my phenomenological healing practice, working with trauma survivors, that the spiritual world has confirmed its existence time and time again. Shamanism's appeal is that it offers an internal support system of tools that experientially and phenomenologically validate the existence of another dimension.

This is not just imagination: this other dimension, or world, is believed to be as real as the chair I am sitting in as I write this. Over the years, as I was looking to expand a skill set that could offer more powerful healing for a population all too familiar with trauma, abuse, pain, and suffering, shamanism, with its emphasis on soul retrieval, revealed itself more fully, with great consistency of positive results. It is not uncommon for folks in difficult circumstances to desire a transcendent experience, a way to rise above the realities of their physical existence. It has been my professional and personal experience that the integration of Gestalt theory/therapy and shamanism has offered a conceptual model that is well defined, accessible, and magical in very practical and powerful yet mystical ways. This is the path I share with you in this book. "Embodied enlightenment" implies that it is in our bodies, and through the medium of our bodies, that we experience the Divine.

The majority of my clients appear in my office when they are moving through times of transition or facing existential crises of despair. Throughout these periods, many of them admit to a curiosity about the existence of something other than or beyond their cognition and their body, the bodymind self. Most understand that there may be a different lens through which to view the circumstances of their lives. Understandably, some of us hold on to more skepticism than do others regarding the potentiality of the existence of soul life—and the idea that our souls may be informing the unfolding of our lives in ways that our rational comprehension cannot quite grasp. Some of us fear judgment from others and the label of "flakiness" if we dare to speak candidly of matters pertaining to our soul. With the initial writing of this manuscript, I fretted far more than I should have about how candid to be. My sons' relentless prodding and encouragement to "write in an uncensored way" what my "soul needed to say" is what it took for me to write this book with this level of honesty.

The background banter in your busy brain right now may be doubtful about my basic assumptions—and that is okay (quite human, I think). What I speak of in these pages may even invite from some the "lunatic" label (you may make this judgment of me, or you may worry that others will make this judgment of you if you confess yourself a believer in such matters). I'd like to suggest a reframing of the term. "Luna" actually refers to the Latin name for the moon and is the same word in both Italian and Spanish. While Western culture has adapted the psychological meaning of "lunatic" to be quite negative, I suggest that we reclaim its original meaning from ancient Rome. Luna, the one who carries the personification of the moon goddess, invites us to commune in greater rhythm with the organic, rhythmic cycles of the moon and perhaps gain greater moon consciousness through this cyclic communion. A connection to the moon's consistent, circular movement supports an intrinsic understanding of the waxing and waning of our days, our energies, our emotional processes—our human process—allowing our actions and minds to be guided, literally, by wisdom and certain basic truths about movement and primordial, sacred rhythm. A "moon consciousness," which Carl Jung wrote about,[4] appreciates that psychological wisdom integrates psyche, the Soul Realm, understanding that our souls dispense light onto the dark shadows of our being—some possibly due to the enduring themes of past lives (this will be discussed further in later chapters).

Understanding that I am foundationally rooted in the somatic psychological theories (mainly Gestalt theory/therapy) and Protestant theological seminary studies may help you maintain an open mind to this material and appreciate the journey "from whence I came." I am not merely pontificating about metaphysical matters from my own personal experience. I have been integrating this material professionally since 1997, observing miracles daily. My years of experience have confirmed that we are all on a journey, collectively, and affirmed the activity of Mystery individually and uniquely—regardless of the religious dogma of a particular path to which we attach ourselves. As Jalaluddin Rumi affirms, "Love is that flame that once kindled burns everything and *only the mystery and the journey remain*" (italics mine).[5] Releasing your rigid attachments to fixed ideas and constricting religious conceptions may help you stay open and receptive to new ideas and fresh experiments. If you come from a particular faith tradition (as I do), you should discover that this information can easily be integrated into your particular faith worldview. Studying at a Christian college myself, steeped in a Protestant model of theological theorizing and praxis—with an understanding that the two are undeniably interconnected—reinforced for me that theorizing and philosophizing about the mysteries of life cannot and must not be separated from practical application.

While reading this book and experimenting with its principles as life tools, you may find yourself taking a lunar leap of faith into an expansive dialogue with Mystery and discovering that Mystery wants to inform the decision making of your life differently that you are typically accustomed to—all the while cultivating a more open, whole heart. As you read, try fostering an inner openness and curiosity about the life of the soul, wondering about its practical application to your life. When you hit your resistance or skepticism or close-mindedness, breathe into it, accepting it, even embracing it, while at the same time talking back to it. Allow any resistance or skepticism to move in and back out, just like an ocean wave. After all, these are simply thoughts passing through the container of your body. Invite yourself to reevaluate your conceptual framework for perceiving reality, perhaps asking new questions on your spiritual quest. While I conceptualize within a solid ground of Gestalt psychology (which values the embracing of polarities and resistances), you, too, might practice holding polarities as aspects of the totality of who you are—the yin/yang of life—visualizing an infinity symbol of movement connecting one pole to the other, your skepticism and your curiosity, your disbelief and your trust.

Psychological theory holds that perception can be understood both constructively and destructively within a spectrum of continuation from light to dark aspects of life—as with the interiority of the self. As beings with will, we are able to choose which decisions to foster. Allow your soul to shed light on your skepticism, if it exists, understanding that this is the process of moving toward greater clarity of understanding the totality of your being, both human and divine. Somewhere in the middle is often the unified place of neutrality and inner balance where divine revelation is free to guide our human actions.

EMBODIED ENLIGHTENMENT

Embodiment precedes enlightenment although enlightenment also precedes embodiment. How's that for a circular paradox? As Plato's writings note, due to the birthing experience and the incarnating, humans have lost most of our souls' memories.[6] Consequently, we need to be reconfigured, first, in these bodies so that our disembodied soul fragments can return home. Whether or not the idea is universally accepted, many different disciplines and diverse world religions affirm that humans spend multiple lifetimes retrieving the enlightenment their lost souls once enjoyed. Our psychological and spiritual task in these physical bodies is to integrate the two, embodiment and enlightenment, but initially this must be done in a linear fashion. Embodiment must occur first so that we can move safely from humanity into divinity, and then we can experience the fully integrated, enlightened, *embodied* state of both divinity and humanity interactively communicating with each other. Mysteriously, the two become one as we come home to the inseparable nature of the truth of our being.

As my wise seventy-something client, whom I will call Joseph, said, "I am on a journey backwards to the beginning." Each of us is on this same sacred pilgrimage back to the beginning. We call it "living life," *journeying, perhaps backwards, to the beginning to more fully comprehend the knowledge of our divine origins.* As we take time for reflection with our very souls, we will see more clearly how the pieces of the puzzle fit together. But we must first learn how to pass through the portal into our soul's revelation.

Fortunately, at a timely transition in my professional work back in 2008, I was graciously offered an opportunity to run therapeutic groups for the University Medical Center of Princeton, namely, Princeton House Behavioral Health. It was a gift that the progressive, visionary psychiatrists and enlightened clinical directors asked me to facilitate spirituality groups using my frame drum. Since the groups were both didactic and experiential in nature, most of what I offered ultimately became the contents of this book. There I was, banging my drum with the chronically mentally ill and the dually diagnosed, chemically addicted patients whom I grew to love. So many of them inspired both my brain and my spirit for the two years I shared with them. Their feedback helped strengthen my belief in this work in my times of self-doubt and skepticism. I thank each one of them for their support and the lessons they taught me about the value of this journey. Much to my surprise, this group became a favorite of many patients and therapists, who reported that it fostered the patients' increase in mood stability and therapeutic insight and an expanded self-love.

These brave patients and many of my private-practice clients have courageously allowed themselves to be penetrated by the Soul Realm. As a psychotherapist in Princeton, New Jersey, a university town, I work with a lot of academicians, many of whom have highly developed critical faculties. For the most part, my client base is made up of respected professionals who enjoy the strength of their solidified cognitions. Over the years my clients have willingly explored other aspects of their being with me. I remember the day when I first brought my frame drum to the office, then gradually added a table drum (which I used as a coffee table initially), and my jembe (all of which I now use interchangeably). The drum would start drumming in the ear of my inner self at a particular time in a therapy session. Initially, I would dialogue with the drum and say, "*No, not now. I have seen this client only a few times. My client is going to think I am nuts and not return.*" I would have this inner dialogue with my drum, simultaneously dialoguing with my client on a purely psychological level, until finally I had the courage to say, "I am hearing the drum and it wants me to drum for you at this time. Would you mind if I drummed for you, and together we can ask your soul for some help, inviting additional clarity from your soul's intelligence?" Fortunately, my clients agreed and came back, session after session, for more shamanic experiences because the results were so compelling.

It is the process of beginning to understand one's self as *soul* that is both exhilarating and surprising, requiring a slow and steady approach of discovery by integrating this new, curious information one step at a time, through the daily, repeated embodied experience. All of us who have "gone there" know that the Soul Realm is alive and real and powerful and truly can be trusted. We also know that when it speaks, we must respond. We begin to understand that our souls will carry us home to the truth of who we are as we learn to flow with the metaphoric current of the ancient river of life (this water element carries innate wisdom and guidance about a life well lived; it will be discussed further in chapters to come).

Some days the current may be rougher than others and we may hit more submerged rocks, but as we learn to trust the river (and the idea of constant movement), we begin to flow with the rhythm of our soul and heighten our awareness about the times when we are not in touch with our own flow. We begin to come home to our soul's full expression and earnest desires, our dream's destiny fulfilled. The "choice-less choice" as Dr. Jean Houston likes to call it, means that we must respond to what our soul knows to be true while sometimes experiencing the judgment and misunderstanding of those who may not fully comprehend. Often the external judgment mimics the internal aspects of the doubting, skeptical self. The reluctance and resistance will be there. It is merely a process of learning to affirm the guidance of our soul's destiny while also learning how to feed this aspect of soul as the one that wins out. Over time, there will be a confidence and self-assurance that our soul is leading us onto the right and necessary path of fulfilling what must be.

The Cosmic Soul—the Soul Realm—(known by many names, the Name among Many Names) can be compared to the vastness of the deep blue sea. We can choose to put on a snorkel and mask and enjoy the beauty from a topical view, experiencing more fleeting moments of soul knowledge while minimally trusting it, or we can plummet to the depths, suiting up with proper gear, perhaps dive suit and tank, to explore the expansiveness of our soul's potential. As we learn to live with this awareness in everyday life, our attention to our soul will become much more connected to our human personality in daily decision making and actions. To do this, we need a daily spiritual practice that gives

XXIV BODY AS SANCTUARY FOR SOUL

us the opportunity to be disciplined about our desire to work with our expanded knowledge—through the experiment of *embodied experience*.

Another way of "suiting up" is to enter into a shamanic state of consciousness. In the world of shamanism we invite the beat of the frame drum, with its consistent primal pulse, to carry us into states of theta brain-wave activity, in which we grab onto the tale of a whale or the fin of a sea turtle, perhaps, and find ourselves more easily accessing our soul's imagery as a primordial mythical time is made present for us in the here-and-now moment. We now know from brain research that vibrations from rhythmic sounds have a profound effect on expanded brain activity, allowing us to reach higher states of creativity, expanded problem-solving ability, and heightened ecstasy and bliss—not unlike the Beatles song "Let It Be": "*When I find myself in times of trouble, Mother Mary comes to me, speaking words of wisdom, let it be.*" It is common in shamanic states to be greeted by a great Ascended Master (like Mother Mary or Jesus or the Buddha) and experience a direct encounter in which messages are delivered, ultimately experiencing ecstasy and/ or ultimate peace. The consistent beat of the frame drum functions as a kind of mantra, fostering deepened sensation and the creation of words, images, and tunes similar to ancient mantras chanted in yoga or meditation practices centuries ago.

As originally understood in both Hinduism and Buddhism, a mantra is a word or sound repeated to aid in concentration, for meditative purposes. A mantra is considered capable of creating spiritual transformation, offering tools to better access an expanded state of consciousness. If we allow ourselves to encounter this type of spiritual discovery through repeated subjective experience with the beat of the drum, we will find ourselves able to talk back, internally, to any fear or skepticism held by the wounded personality about exploring our soul's depths. With consistency of daily, disciplined practice, we will open to the Soul Realm with greater trust and devotion. As we practice these tools daily, hidden and undeniable sacred truths will be revealed. These nuggets that unveil themselves are intimately acquainted with what holds the deepest meaning for our true nature—usually what we hold most private and dear is known by our soul, and our soul responds to it with a particular preciseness that is undeniably affirming. Our souls promise to elevate and enlighten us with their knowledge (if we let them); their wisdom will be from a much different perspective from this material realm yet will still hold applicability to this earthly life. Harnessing this sacred gnosis, saving knowledge, either as daily spiritual practice or as an addition to one's repertoire of healing practices, is central in many mystical traditions. It is our soul's consciousness that holds the promise of pure potentiality of being, what is referred to in psychological theory as the potential for "self-actualization." Unfortunately, it appears all too common in human nature for the ego to attach itself to the resistance of our soul's unveiling and to fight this process of our soul's direct revelation, falsely believing that authoritative others know better than we do about the state of our own soul. Most of us know all too well the struggle we humans endure to be born and to be birthed into our true nature, our soul.

UNDERSTANDING MORE ABOUT FEAR AS IMMOBILIZING

Swami Brahmdev, in his book, *Questions and Answers*, discusses fear in a practical yet powerful way. Brahmdev states that "one of the remedies to conquer fear is to face with courage what one fears, and like that fear disappears. What is unknown always gives us a sensation of fear. Fear is a negative imagination of our mind which invents what has not happened and makes us fear things that will probably never happen. Another remedy is to have faith in the Divine; if we are confident that the best happens for us always, we will never fear."[7] Clearly, it is courage that answers back to fear, and courage needs internal daily *encouragement*. Similar sentiments were popularized by Will Smith's character in the movie *After Earth*:

> Fear is not real. The only place that fear can exist is in our thoughts of the future. It is a product of our imagination, causing us to fear things that do not at present, and may not ever, exist. That is near insanity. Do not misunderstand me. Danger is very real but fear is a choice. We are all telling ourselves a story.

How then do we understand fear so that we are not disowning or suppressing it yet, at the same time, are giving it minimal respect? Fear is rooted in a paradigm, a narrative, of constriction and protection contained by the part of our personality that is attached to our human woundedness and our limitation. While sometimes we need fear to alert us to danger that is real, we need to practice distinguishing between fear that is useful and fear that is not, remembering that *the soul does not know fear.* It should be expected, initially, that you will repeatedly encounter moments of fear, panic, and anxiety as you find yourself curious about exploring more deeply the realm of Sacred Mystery, wondering what it might ask of you. Remembering that your soul understands that fear ought not have the final word, we begin to support an internal dialogue between our wounded self (who holds the fear) or our egocentric self (who holds an arrogant superiority) and our soul (who holds an openness—a desire to come home). It is important that we make a deliberate and conscious choice for something other than the fear to win out. Faith talks back to fear. Love talks back to fear. Curiosity talks back to fear. Many aspects of our willful self, while embracing our power to act, talk back to the fear and its power to shut down our receptivity. Love, vulnerability, faith, authenticity, and courage inhabit the Soul Realm. As we begin to understand this process conceptually, we learn to constantly and consistently support this internal dialogue between the fear and faith, doubt and trust, skepticism and courage, constriction and openness. To embrace both polarities of feeling and learn to hold them in the container of our bodies is human. To support the action of faith, trust, and receptivity is divine. Repeated shamanic experience will reinforce a knowing with certainty and a belief in the power of this work and lead us to trust the guidance from the voice of the soul.

Over the years, thousands of my clients have attested to the credibility and depth of this soul-retrieval work; but they can say this only because they have allowed themselves, repeatedly, to have shamanic experiences—not just to debate these concepts on an intellectual level. This work is not superficial. Quite the contrary, the work of soul retrieval, soul healing, and soul journeying is vast, timeless, and magical. It is possible that you may feel fearful of the information initially retrieved, even for years after embarking on this discovery (as has been true for me and many of my clients). Know that your soul does not want you to be afraid; that would limit the power of the work and veil your soul's ascension. If you find yourself feeling afraid at any point while reading this book, stop and attend to your fear. Begin an inner dialogue within, in which you allow your fear and your soul to exchange differing points of view, making sure that your soul has the last word; in other words, the soul wants to be "top dog." I promise you that your soul will always want to answer back to your fear. Your soul and your soul guides will be right there, by your side, to help you interpret whatever information is revealed to you.

Remember, if you make it known that you seek healing—to be released from the wounds of your physical/psychological body—and are asking that your being be reconfigured in the ancient knowing of your soul's memory of its true nature, it will be done. One step at a time, one healing fragment at a time, will bring you closer and closer to a peaceful experience of "home" in your body. You will have an internal experience that is real, alive, and direct in its message's application for your specific need. Over time, you will begin to trust this process, as you will experience your soul's truth and power, precise in its timeliness to your need. Any skepticism or doubt you may carry about this practice will be answered through the experience you allow yourself to have. To open up to an experience with the Soul Realm, it is essential to practice receptivity—a belief in the concept that there may be something more than reality as we presently perceive it.

Simply put, our souls remind us that *we once remembered what we think we now forget;* hence the term "the cosmic return." Our earthly pilgrimage tries to stomp out our flame, but our soul holds the memory of our flame's refusal to be extinguished permanently. Our soul desires permission to talk back to our human woundedness and somehow manage to reignite the flame of truth. For the soul knows that the Larger Flame burns always for us; the circle circles for us humans in some enduring way (as sun and moon remind us of the constancy of this enlightenment). A shamanic practice teaches us that the Drum drums for us, refusing to lay its drumstick down, in the hopes that we might remember who we are through our soul's lens.

If my writing is resonating somewhere inside, even if it is that still, quieter voice within, know this to be true for yourself; and if your soul recognizes the truth of my words, then you are a soul seeker of mystery—a mystic—like me, eager to go more deeply into the realm of the sacred mysteries, and this is the right book for you. The topics in this book will resonate with those of you who are beginners on this path or those of you who are already on a spiritual path yet seeking something more.

"More what?" you may be asking. Only you can answer that question; that is the dialogue to engage in with your soul's protectors and your soul guides. I imagine that you seek more practical knowledge of some sort, specific to your soul's purpose in the world. Or perhaps you are interested in seeing your soul in its different incarnations so that you will have a better sense of its enduring themes and core essence. Or you may already have a basic understanding of your soul's enduring themes and want to help your soul re-create a more actualized life that is not interrupted by roadblocks from past lives. Designed for all sorts of spiritual seekers, this book will welcome both your curiosity and your skepticism as you bring all of who you are, authentically and without judgment, allowing yourself to delve with curiosity and receptivity into the depths of a conscious understanding and connect with your very soul.

INTRODUCTION
Reaching Transcendence

> *The soul never thinks without an image.*
>
> ARISTOTLE

While meditation is designed to quiet the busy brain, the meditative state need not be accessed through stillness only. There are many meditative activities that lead us toward enlightenment or transcendence through active movement. Yoga can enhance a meditative or transcendent state, even though it is rooted in activity, *asanas*. Walks in nature can also enhance a transcendent state. Experiencing art in its many different forms, such as ecstatic dance, is also meditative and can awaken us to our bliss even though we are not sitting in stillness on the floor. This raises the question, *What is transcendence?* How is it defined? Can someone who makes a three-point shot in the last five seconds of a basketball game reach a transcendent state as the ball goes swoosh into the net? Or, when you are having a fabulous conversation with someone you dearly love, are you reaching transcendence? Have you ever wondered why so many children are preoccupied with a desire to fly? When kids are younger and still inhabiting the active life of their imagination, taking flight is a daily magical conversation. Are we instinctively wired to yearn for that which is transcendent? To your soul, transcendence is all there is.

WHAT IS SHAMANISM?

The transformative mystical path that provides tools to access ecstasy and transcendence is the ancient, cross-cultural practice of shamanism. Through shamanism we merge with the universal, cosmic energetic pulse; the beat of the heart. The beat of the frame drum provides an opening into the awakening of the heart center while also offering internal healing—known as medicine—delivered direct from Spirit. This practice—which becomes a way of life—can help us thrive during

1

the many shifts and changes that life brings to us, regardless of the tumultuous circumstances we may encounter. With this practice, we access an altered state of consciousness, ecstatic transcendence, in which we potentially commune with the realm of Holy Mystery. By "ecstatic transcendence," I mean a type of trance that is associated with ecstasy or bliss (which, again, is the only communication the soul knows). In this expanded state of consciousness, we can enter an inner world that few people are consciously familiar with. In these simple shamanic practices, we learn a skill set that helps to improve our lives; we learn to ride gracefully through life's constant vicissitudes. This is a strange, dreamlike world where we work in partnership with many helping spirits; amazingly, reports of the structure of this world from shamans of different times and places—from Siberia and Central Asia, where shamanism was first observed, to North and South America, Indonesia, Tibet, China, and beyond—are strikingly similar in their details. In cultures with shamanic traditions, shamans (who hold the central position in the community) may cure illness and restore personal power, divine the future, locate food, appease restless spirits, influence weather, and give guidance to the people of their community. Being in this world is something like entering a dream while awake and consciously deciding what to do there. Mysteriously, this world is invisible (and just out of reach) to people's "normal" daytime mind, but as you learn to move into a shamanic state of consciousness, you will learn to trust that it is just as real and informative.

Even though I have been integrating shamanism and psychology since 1996, I still see myself as a novice in comprehending the complexities of the life of the soul. In this pursuit of gnosis, or inner knowledge, I align myself with the mission of the shamans and the mystics, ageless in the pursuit of sacred wisdom and healing while within the body. The integration of both a solid psychological theory of the self and an integrated methodology of the soul is essential in understanding the complexity and mystery of the Soul Realm.

Much of what I write about regarding the validity of soul activity is privately believed by many but not often publicly discussed or affirmed—often due to believers' fear of being judged, shamed, or marginalized. I know this to be true from the confidential work I have done over the years with many professionals and university academics. Take, for example, a

Harris poll that finds that 72 percent of the US population believes in angels.[1] In 2009, the Pew Research Center reported that nearly one in five Americans experienced ghosts and one in seven had consulted a psychic.[2] While many Americans may not talk about their personal relationship with the metaphysical world, this research suggests that many may be engaging in some sort of dialogue with the supernatural, apart from any religious affiliation, and indeed are obsessed with the notion. In the Bible (Matthew 18:10), Jesus tells his disciples that children have their "angels in heaven." This verse has encouraged many Protestants and Catholics alike to believe that each of us has a watchful guardian angel protecting us—one we can even pray to for aid with specific requests. Many Christian theologies teach that angels know everything and that what is known only to God is confidentially carried on their wings. Understandably, many humans look to these celestial beings for aid with the struggles of daily life, believing that angels carry certain powers into which humans can tap. Yet many do not share this information in daily conversation with one another. Some folks might choose to engage more with their protective angels and spirit helpers if these sorts of topics became less "off-limits" and more mainstream.

As I was not raised Catholic, I have a limited understanding about the saints in the Catholic Church. I understand that they are believed to be bestowed with mediatory, magical powers, similar to the abilities that shamanic animal spirits and soul guides use to help us when we are in shamanic states of consciousness. This suggests that there may be other divine beings whose knowledge of the "secret code" is far greater than ours here on the physical plane, limited by these bodies of flesh. Think about St. Joseph, "the real estate agent." How many people do you know who have buried a statue of Saint Joseph in their front garden to assist in selling their houses more expediently, only to find out that, in fact, it worked and the results were fast? Or so the stories go. But these stories are the same around the globe. The power of Saint Joseph is as real in my husband's small hometown village of Miranda, Italy, as it is here in New Jersey, where my local real estate agent suggested I bury his statue for quicker results.

Whatever your faith tradition (even if the sun, moon, and stars are your religion), each of us has a unique story that has deeply impacted our curiosity with the soul's power to aid and illuminate. This book will highlight these private moments of dialogue with the Soul Realm, of harnessing its miraculous medicinal powers, while inviting this conversation to become public so that the seed of conversation about the Soul Realm may be spread, effecting change throughout the world to create a soulful society. What I offer is a fluid form for the exploration with Spirit in the play, the curiosity about your own soul. To remain open to and curious about the play within the form is essential.

As the Trappist monk Thomas Merton noted, "To live life without this illuminated consciousness is to live as a Beast of Burden. The weight of the burden is the seriousness with which one takes one's own individual and separate self. To live with the true consciousness of life centered in Another is to lose one's self-important seriousness and thus to live life as "play" in union with a Cosmic Player."[3] In this case, "Another" is our soul dialoguing with the Cosmic Soul, the Soul Realm.

CHAPTER 1
PSYCHOLOGY, SHAMANISM, AND THE SOUL REALM

Any life-form in any realm—mineral, vegetable, animal, or human—can be said to undergo "enlightenment." It is, however, an extremely rare occurrence since it is more than an evolutionary progression: It also implies a discontinuity in its development, a leap to an entirely different level of Being and, most important, a lessening of materiality.

ECKHART TOLLE

Due to the influence of rationalism and its constrictions, psychology (with the exception of the Jungian analysis), as a discipline, has thus far proved itself limited in accessing psyche's (the soul's) information. Much in the field of psychology has lost its own soul and therefore does not provide a means of helping clients to access psyche with a practical, clear methodology. Much religious dogma has also failed to offer an in-depth, practical understanding of the life of the soul. Therefore, the development of an innovative, clear, and integrative model synthesizing both psychology and soulful philosophies becomes even more necessary. Psychology teaches us to ground, to boundary, to physically embody, and to individuate, becoming a solid, permeable yet impermeable self. This can feed an emphasis on ego, as ego-strength is foundational to a fully individuated self capable of making healthy contact with the external environment.

Spirituality, on the other hand, reminds us that our spirits seek inspiration to soar, inviting us to let go of our solid, impermeable, individualized self, releasing us into ecstatic union so that we can merge into cosmic oneness with the expansive unseen universe—the larger whole. The invitation from the Soul Realm is to release the development of this egocentric self and, in fact, to allow the soul to manifest its truest potential as the primary expression of the personality while at the same time fulfilling the mission of the Cosmic Soul. Mysteriously, there is constantly a fruitful tension of one reality informing the other, body/ soul, physical/spiritual, form/formless, as we evolve and transform into higher potentiality of consciousness. Rooted in both earth and sky worlds simultaneously, as human spirits, physical/spiritual beings, we receive from our soul's unfolding information that potentially shapes how we relate to our physical earth and sky realities. The soul is that aspect of us which instinctively understands this and carries the seed of memory about the truth of who we are and the truth of our purpose in this life. Once we align with this knowledge, we will live a life of greater fulfillment, satisfaction, and service to the broader mission. The challenge is to learn to weed out the distractions, doubts, and confusion (created by the human, wounded imprint) so that the tiny seed of memory can reveal itself and take form.

Gestalt therapy/theory's insistence on the body's kinesthetic intelligence, and shamanism's "release-and-retrieval" methods—release of the human limitations and retrieval of the soul's perception—are both models rooted in phenomenological evidence. These ancient methods provide a practical model for living each moment present in the body while consciously attached and connected with the soul. Interestingly, both models are rooted in the concept of phenomenology, which basically means that individual perception and conscious awareness of subjective experience as experiment is validated from the first-person point of view; it is a basic phenomenological tenet that what I say is in fact *true because* "*my experience leads me to say so*." As we become aware of our own inner world of thoughts, emotions, sensation, and "higher-mind mindfulness" (call it intuition, gnosis, instinct, imagination, spiritual perception), we become more capable of accessing and discerning our body's intelligence and our soul's consciousness—clarity, truth, and healing—learning to depend on ourselves as authoritative enough to become *the final authority of what's best for our own being*. Gestalt theory/therapy refers to this concept as "self-organismic regulation."

This calls into question the necessity for external authority figures who seek to be the gurus of our personal decision making—whether they be psychotherapists, priests, psychics, yoga teachers, or otherwise—all of whom can inadvertently diminish our personal power and the validity of our own subjective truth. Certainly, I am not denying the utility of these guiding professions and, in fact, I believe in the importance of their existence in society—after all, I am a part of the psychotherapist pastoral tribe! My concern arises when we create such dependence on external authority figures that we lose touch with our own soul's knowledge and its innate ability to guide us. Others become the authoritative guides for our own lives and our own beliefs as we subtly dismiss our soul's inner voice. The key is to learn to stay focused inward and not to cede authority to external influences, despite the temptation to yield to those we deem to be more knowledgeable than ourselves. We must learn to understand that external figures, however well-intentioned they may be, can keep us detached from our inner soul's knowing as authoritative truth. We each have the capacity to be guided by our own soul as "the Authority" in its own right. This may be similar to asking an external other (a psychotherapist or a member of the clergy) to give us information, but instead the information comes from within our own wellspring of attachment to our soul. Essentially, each of us has the capability to be our own mediator and advisor, to channel the Divine, to follow the knowing of our soul's true expression. The challenge is to learn to listen inside and to act on what we know to be true according to our soul. *There is no better teacher than your own soul.* This is the truest guide there is. This book will teach you a practical skill set that will enable you to merge with your soul as your primary guide, as you learn to safely inhabit your body and embrace both the finite and the Infinite in this physical container.

GESTALT THEORY:
BODY INTELLIGENCE AS A BRIDGE OF ACCESS TO THE DIVINE

As a body-centered psychotherapy, among the somatic psychologies, Gestalt theory is my preferred psychological modality for guiding a going-inward process, because of its insistence on body awareness as the very simple goal of therapy. Simple awareness of the bodymind, rooted in the body's innate intelligence, holds the powerful potential to teach us a skill set for positively and constructively managing both our cognition and our emotion. We then become a more conscious sentient being by paying attention to sensation in the body. One of Gestalt theory's primary tenets is the concept of "external and internal supports" in daily life. The basic idea is that an experience of internal validation, void of the poison of self-doubt, holds incredible opportunity to access more of the kernel of the truth of authentic self, or true nature, or soul. Internal supports, which are heightened through shamanic journeying experience, for example, function as an internal structure, or pillar, for inner strength and courage, which, by necessity, will foster a deeper connection with and trust of the self, from the inside out. This means that the soul will begin to feel safe to reveal itself because the internal structure has a solid foundation with solid pillars to hold itself up. It is necessary for an organism to inhabit this psychological safety in the body in order to self-regulate and move toward one's own excitement and need and evolve into the full maturity of one's age.

In other words, the more we have constructive inner supportive structures for our soul's true expression, the greater our level of integrated health, inner peace, and aliveness. We are then able to foster and cultivate external systems or communities of support and validation in the broader world—which will offer us greater external support for the continual unfolding of our soul's path. This ends up being *one big, broad cosmic breath*—the giving and receiving of the pulse of the sacred universe unfolding as it should. We learn that we can inhale and exhale, take in and move out, retrieve and release, trusting the reciprocity of the rhythmic flow of life's interdependent web. We learn through experience, regardless of the circumstances that life sends our way, that the physical and spiritual aspects of life are intertwined and are playmates supporting our soul's ascension.

Using a psychological framework, specifically Gestalt theory, we learn to value paying attention from the inside out, while being aware of bodily sensation, as the initial step in moving toward organismic self-regulation. What this means is that there is hope for all of us to learn how to create psychological safety for ourselves inside these physical containers—or cylinders—our bodies. Once we are no longer living in a fight/flight/freeze, survival mentality, we can move toward a more elevated consciousness. As we learn to foster mood stability and emotional regulation, we understand that we have the capacity to support a healthy self-management of all that we feel and think. This inner awareness feeds a capacity for clarity (versus confusion) and freedom (versus entrapment) and authenticity (versus a role). As you, a healthy organism, learn to support yourself in moving toward that which your soul needs and desires, you experience yourself living the life you want and finding fulfillment and purpose. Using the tools to feed repetitive experiences that are pleasant and positively rewarding, versus unpleasant, will foster a daily sense of autonomy and control over constructive thoughts, feelings, and actions—"those things which I can control," to use the 12-step lingo. Confidence and self-reliance will grow as you learn to trust, in both your inner and your outer worlds, that you can find what you need in the "environmental field" because you now have the skills to do so.

Obviously, we don't really have a choice in what we initially feel and think. Part of being human is that we learn to embrace what we initially experience. Like robots, most of us have learned to react, unconsciously feeding the wounded imprint to develop habitual behavioral patterns. We learn, however, as we grow in health, that *we do have a choice in how long we allow any destructive cognition and destructive emotion to gestate in our bodies*. We do learn that *we have a choice whether or not to allow our emotions to dictate actions that could lead to self-destructive patterns*. We can learn through practicing soul-awareness that we are capable of becoming more conscious and acting in a more enlightened way toward self and others. This kind of practical enlightenment is both embodied and relational.

A daily practice of soul attachment feeds inspiration from above, creativity, rather than reactivity (which comes from the wounded human imprint). We also learn to nurture our self-confidence by talking back internally to any self-doubt and lack of trust. Mastery and self-agency of our bodies allows us to live in our bodies and feed psychological safety. We no longer feel the necessity to react and reinforce wounded aspects of our personality and retraumatize ourselves or retrigger unpleasant emotional states that leave us feeling at the mercy of others (and detached from our very soul). Such destructive patterns can feed a betrayal and abandonment of the self. When this occurs it does not feel okay to inhabit our own skin. As we use this consciousness to elevate and transform our cognition, affect, and behaviors, we begin to feel a more permanent attachment to our soul because our soul feels safe enough to live at home in the vessel of the body.

Sensation is the gateway to this initial pathway inward, which leads us toward a deepened awareness of body, mind, and potentially, soul. Moment to moment we learn to practice what is called in the field of mindfulness "presence," which is another word for compassionate awareness without judgment or rational-brain censorship. Once we

Due to cultural conditioning, many of us have internalized a dualistic model that fosters an unconscious separation from our body. We have been conditioned to live in accordance with the introjects* from the "interruptive influences of the environmental fields," such as family, society, culture, or organized religion. In systems that require us to play a role (as opposed to being authentic) as a requirement for membership, we often lose touch with our inner voice of truth and consequently live separated from our bodies. The various systems often communicate, verbally and nonverbally, a need for interruptive responses in order to get the needs of the systems met. Frequently, that which is expected of us supersedes our real and genuine individual needs.

Enduring interruptive states create dualities of self (as Joyce's quote depicts), as well as splits in the internal body (which can actually be seen upon closer scrutiny of the way in which each body holds itself, as the diagram shows). After years of observing bodies in my therapeutic practice, I continue to be amazed at the manner in which they hold memory, visible to the physical eye. According to the Somatic Psychologies, body splits are an adaptive response to life's disruptive experiences. These interruptions, memories of which are stored in the body, foster dis-regulation. As a product of fragmented aspects of the self, these splits usually function unnoticed, interrupting a balanced flow of internal wholeness. Socialized expectations that emphasize "external locus of control" (as opposed to internal locus of control) contribute to the self being a false self, a role of what others' need, feeding a disconnection with one's true nature, the soul. If these internal body splits remain fragmented and divided, it will be difficult if not impossible to access internal unification, and you will find yourself creating your internal state in the external world. A shamanic state of consciousness constantly applies its medicine to heal these internal dualities and interruptive energies through extraction techniques, releasing the immobilizing energies that are constricting the life-force energy flow.

In his book *BodyMind*, Ken Dychtwald discusses the five basic body splits.[2] These internal splits carry ramifications, internally as well as

---

* "Introjection" as a Gestalt term is an interrupted state that functions to separate us from our own sensation, which is the portal inward to remain in good contact with the authentic, spontaneous, alive self.

(5) Major Body/Mind Splits

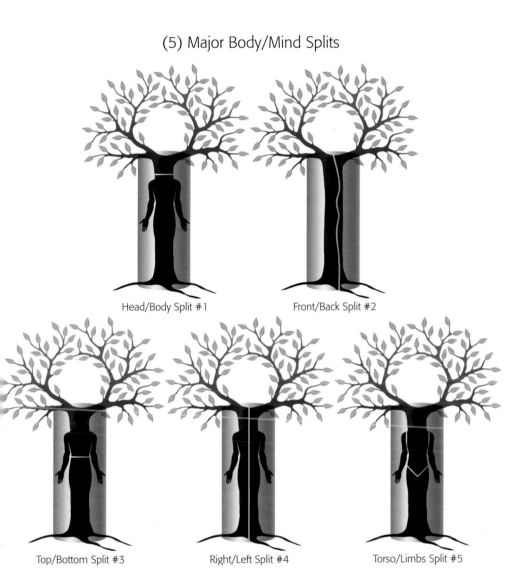

Head/Body Split #1   Front/Back Split #2

Top/Bottom Split #3   Right/Left Split #4   Torso/Limbs Split #5

externally, as they are acted out in the environmental field, characterizing relational divisions and fragmentation. For communities and relationships to exist harmoniously, the individual's inner world must be unified and at peace. In thinking about these internal body splits, it is useful to imagine your body as a cylinder with a front, a back, and sides. Ideally, we are working to unify our cylinder into connective experiences so that all aspects of the self are working together. We are all too familiar with the typical separation that we experience between our heads and our bodies. (Each of the above diagrams matches a particular split.)

❖ **Head/Body Split #1:** This split occurs in people who "live in their heads" and cannot quiet their busy brains, even when they want to. These people perceive themselves to be their thoughts and are quite content to live a short distance from their bodies. Cognition reigns supreme and their critical faculties are not in balance with their emotional awareness nor their soul's expression. These people experience themselves as their rational brain only—with minimal or no awareness as to how cut off they are from their own body sensation.

❖ **Front/Back Split #2:** This is the split between the front side and the back side of the body; for example, pain in the heart will often coincide with tightness in the trapezius muscle in the back/shoulder area. As this split is healed, this person will realize the way in which their solid yet flexible spine supports their open heart, for example. They will become more aware of moving through the world with a whole heart, while their backbone will sustain a groundedness and rootedness as primary supportive structure. The feet will feel more rooted and solid, as the heels and the toes are evenly distributed in the ground of earth. This balance will also support the way in which they move forward into the world with an open heart yet also "feel their own back," meaning that they are able to protect themself appropriately with healthy boundaries and "have their own back."

❖ **Top/Bottom Split #3:** This is the split between the top trunk and the lower trunk, occurring around the belly and the hips. When this split is operational, the root will not be connected to the rest of the body and this person will find themself acting in ways that are incongruous —the heart not connected to the head, the head not connected to the feet, and one's movement not connected to truth, clarity, and authenticity of being. Basically, imbalance, incongruence, and inauthenticity will abound and this person's experience in the world will be of not belonging.

❖ **Right/Left Split #4:** This is the split between the left side of the body, the sacred feminine (the receiving aspect) and the right side of the body, the sacred masculine (the giving aspect). It causes a lack of integration and imbalance in sun/moon consciousness. Sun/moon consciousness, when functioning in balance, allows one to be connected to personal power while integrating the wisdom from the unseen universe (the third eye, of intuition), experiencing the interconnectedness of all living beings, and materializing soul's purpose in the middle world. This inner experience of holism will provide a different way of moving through the external world. Power to act, strength of will, and courage to express will be bright; being seen in all your fullness, embodying spontaneity and authenticity humbly, will be expressed as a manifestation of your true nature, your soul. When this balance is complete, the solar plexus is full and radiant like the sun. This energy radiates inward first, filling the internal body, then radiates outward, moving this energy out into the larger world.

❖ **Torso/Limbs Split #5:** This is the split between the trunk and the limbs, which often feeds a lack of spatial and body awareness typical of disembodiment. This person may be more accident-prone, and relationship splits will be more apparent in the outside world, this person having a greater propensity to foster divisive communication and splitting behaviors in the larger community because their movement is not connected to an open heart.

You don't have a soul. You are a soul. You have a body.

C. S. Lewis

The diagrams below detail a graphic image of the body perceived as cylindrical, both internally and externally (with a top, a bottom, a front, a back, and two sides). This self-perception allows for an internal image that includes an energetic pull toward our core—an inner, aligned, and connected center. This visual imagery can help us answer back to a compartmentalized image of the body. When we add to this by layering upon another image, we imagine our skeletal structure from

In Divinity's Embrace, Duality Unifies

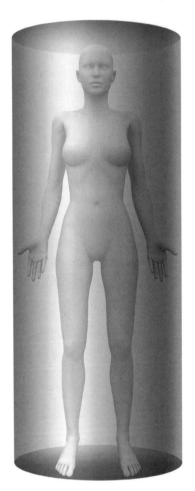
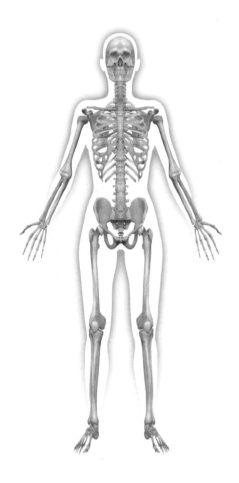

within, realizing that this inner perception can sometimes help us utilize renewed visualizations as a powerful healing tool. We begin to understand that we are designed to function in a connected way; that both sturdiness of structure *and* fluidity of movement are inherent in our physical design. Learning to embrace and respect the balance of these two polarities on a physical level also invites us to embrace these aligned and balanced energies psychologically.

BETSY FINDS HER BACKBONE

Elizabeth, whom many call Betsy, is a professional woman in her mid-fifties, married with three grown children. She was a newcomer to psychotherapy, and it came as a shock to her when she realized that she had never utilized her backbone in relationship to others. Her role of accommodation, yielding to other's needs, was becoming more than she could bear in her mid-life years. Secretly, she knew exactly what she wanted and needed but found herself unable to speak her truth in the relationships of her life. Her own clarity about this only made it worse for her. Her self-blame and self-hatred were severe, as she could not take risks to go after what she really wanted. As she and I did some guided imagery together while I beat the simple, supportive drumbeat, she awakened in her inner vision to active visual imagery of her own backbone becoming sturdier. She said that she actually felt it solidifying and that, for the first time ever, she could actively imagine herself supporting her inner trunk with some semblance of solidarity. Perceiving herself as an ancient, wise willow tree allowed her to imagine herself staying open to others' movements while moving with the wind and yet remaining rooted in herself. She experienced herself deeply rooted in the earth, not dismissing her own needs and wants as less important. As she imagined herself leaving our session and returning to the challenging relationships of her life, she felt greater internal support and potential ability to stand up for herself in a way that felt more honoring to her.

When we perceive ourselves as both cylindrical and Tree of Life, we become capable of viewing our bodies as holding the historical memory of our chronological selves (in our bones, our blood, our connective tissue, our cells) in a way that depicts connectivity, not fragmentation, with the varied aspects of who we are as a self. This body/mind awareness encompasses all the years that we have lived and moved in these physical bodies as cylinders. Broadly speaking, each stage of our lives holds memory, reinforcing certain rigid beliefs and primary repetitive emotional states; in psychological terminology, we call these "maladaptive behavioral patterns." These habitual patterns are often reinforced by the limited, wounding environments in which we grew up. If we do not get a handle on these interruptions, they will function as roadblocks, interfering with our ability to fully actualize our soul's potential in this lifetime. Because we are always finding ways to get along in this challenging world—through our creative adaptations—our bodies find inventive ways to split into dualistic selves. Often without our conscious awareness, our duality fosters an inner locking or holding onto the emotional memory of past pain, trauma, woundedness, and division. Somewhere inside the container of the body (this somewhere may be in tiny crevices in the connective tissue of our body and/or cells, or it may be that fragments of our soul have splintered off out into the cosmos somewhere) lives the narrative of our life story, embedded and imprinted yet waiting to be healed. Usually this drama all occurs apart from our body/mind consciousness. In Gestalt terms, we refer to this as "creative adaptation," our best attempt to humanly respond to whatever difficulty arises—often at great cost to our inner experience of peace, wholeness, and constant attachment to our soul. Our soul's fragmenting off somewhere is often a way of surviving or enduring painful human experiences.

In the healing process, we learn to thank our bodies for the way in which they have creatively endured our challenging and sometimes abusive circumstances. As we heal, we call home these lost aspects of self and soul that have fragmented off or lain dormant in hiding somewhere, buried deep inside. We begin to understand that these body splits unify our lost (or disowned) parts of self, from the inside out. The more we bring compassionate, loving presence to ourselves, especially reconnecting with our younger selves (ages five through nine), who hold the gift of reclaimed spontaneity, purity, openness, and freedom, the more liberated we become. It is absolutely essential to reconnect with our younger selves within and to understand the core beliefs and affect states they remain attached to. As we learn to reclaim them, embracing them in all their truth, we learn how to reparent our younger aspects of self and begin to understand that these younger aspects hold a belief in the magico-mystical world. The one in charge, reparenting the younger self, is the age that you are.

This unification leads to psychological safety inside your cylinder and reduces confusion when the different parts of self spar or debate within.

As we deepen in our understanding of answering back to the cognitive dissonance or the body's internal duality, we begin to observe our soul emerging as the central "me", the truth of "who I am." We begin to understand and support this aspect of self as the one who holds the final word inside. New beliefs talk back to old beliefs, and past life interruptions are consciously healed in the space of this interaction. You may find, through practicing yoga and practicing shamanism, or by working with any of the body psychotherapies (e.g., massage or Reiki), that you will become more aware of where these body splits reside in your body's interiority. If you are of the Christian faith, the ritual of Communion, with Jesus's emphasis on "the new covenant in my blood, this do in remembrance of me" (I Corinthians 11:25) may hold symbolic significance, reminding you of the importance of our bodies and their interiority as a locality for healing. The focus of the application of this book's material becomes the interior unification of these dichotomous splits, which are often accessed by paying attention to subtlety, nuance, sensation, and color in the inner space. This internal healing will allow you to function more as one, from the inside out. It is my hope that, as each individual person applies this practice, the greater community will function as one communal, connected, compassionate body.

THE DRUMBEAT OF YOUR SOUL—
PRIMORDIAL, SACRED RHYTHM REMEMBERED

The seemingly invisible realm of Soul will become visible as we learn to recognize the subtle signs enveloping us everywhere, both within the natural world and from the internal voice of our true nature. Soul revelation is potentially unfolding, moment to moment, inside the sanctuary of our very bodies. Yet, until we awaken, we fail to have eyes to see or ears to hear the soul's content (much less discern it) unraveling from a constant universe ever seeking to inform our existence. The cultural and societal drumbeat often overpowers the inner beat of our soul's clear message. My intention is to provide a modern-day, practical guide for you to access your soul's drumbeat, by providing guidance through the ancient yet abiding cross-cultural practice of shamanism. The beat of the drum provides the practitioner with theta brain-wave patterns, luring us away from the monkey mind, to aid in creating transcendence so that what we are truly seeking in our core, *our soul*, can emerge from darkness into light. It is not uncommon for most beginners in this practice to hit "blackness" and become afraid (conjuring up religious introjects of the devil, evil, or some other monster of sorts). The black color is merely the reminder of the impasse, the void, the creation waiting to be birthed by the light, into creativity. Sit with the darkness, trusting that the light will emerge and shower its rays of enlightenment, eventually fostering lightness of being, a luminous self, which is the soul peering through.

The soul's direct embodiment, or incarnation, is necessary so that the soul can reveal itself through the medium of the flesh, the physical. Our true natures, our souls, as well as the world of nature, reveal the mysteriousness of the unseen world being made seen, the invisible becoming visible. The soul seems eager to live both *in* the container of the body and still connected to that which is *beyond* the body—that which is uncontainable, that which is infinite. We see in the union of body and soul a depiction of great Mystery, of polarities unified. The body, our physical house, seems to be the vessel of choice, or safe container, our soul seeks. Paradoxically, the soul seeks the physical experience, while the body seeks the spiritual experience. The body and the soul are mysteriously inseparable, in a curious dependence on each other.

David Bohm, a quantum physicist, coined the term "the non-fragmentary worldview," which offers us a lens through which to consider this material: the seen universe and the unseen one—the visible and invisible worlds—as a whole, not two separate worlds rooted in a model of duality but actually one. As systems theory attests, the whole is different from the sum of its parts. *What if* these bodies we inhabit are deeply connected to an immortal, spiritual soul that connects us to a hidden universe—more hidden than our minds can fully comprehend?

This "what if" question is central to the material of this book. *What if* your soul holds information to share with you and is waiting for you to awaken so that it may reveal its secrets to you? In order to access sacred information related to this sort of question, we need to reconsider what we've been told and adjust the socio-cultural lens through which we view this material. The questions then become, how do I do this? Where is my tool kit to access my own soul? How do I access my how-to manual to comprehend the Soul Realm? And how do I water this seed of memory so that my soul will reside fully and completely in my body and I will experience great interconnectedness with the Cosmos?

SHAMANISM: A CONTEMPORARY MAGICO-MYSTICAL, EMBODIED ENLIGHTENMENT PRACTICE

Unfortunately, in Western culture there appears to be a lack of confidence in the institution of religion. Many have been hurt and disappointed by religious communities functioning destructively—which usually happens when they attach themselves to dogma in some rigid way. As people begin to search for meaningful pluralistic spiritual paths and pursue interests related to the soul and the Soul Realm, one practice that offers firsthand experience of knowledge and direct revelation from the world of Spirit is shamanism.

After integrating shamanism with psychotherapy in 1996, I came up with my working definition: shamanism is "a magico-mystical meditative practice that offers a bridge of access to the Soul Realm and must be experienced firsthand to be understood." Mircea Eliade, a University of Chicago religious historian who wrote about shamanism, suggested that shamanism might be better classified among the mysticisms than with what is commonly called a religion.[3]

In mainstream American culture, shamanism has been marginalized from its typical central position within the community (cross-culturally)—in part due to the Western views of shamanism as primitive, superstitious, or backward and outdated, as well as organized religious influences rooted in monotheistic systems of theological doctrine. Fortunately, the rediscovery of shamanism is emerging as a major thrust in the spiritual reawakening of the Western world. Perhaps due to the fast-paced, modern technological world that invades us all daily, we seek methods to escape into altered states of consciousness to see more clearly with the wisdom mind and experience a respite from so many demands. My interest is to revitalize shamanism, more as an *integrated* mysticism and a pathway toward a more *pluralistic* religion, which can also function as a meditative spiritual practice while integrating your particular faith tradition. As a tool, its specific methodology is a guide for accessing the Soul Realm and remembering, as Plato attests, *what has seemingly been forgotten*. Shamanism offers extraordinary methods for accessing hidden dimensions of reality and can connect us with inner sources of power, clarity, and support. This middle world is seen as a reality infused with hidden realities. This means that, as human spirits rooted in both earth and sky, we can access both ordinary and nonordinary states of consciousness.

Contemporary neo-shamanic practices do exist—and are on the rise in the United States—synthesizing and drawing primarily from the field of anthropology, reinventing shamanism in a modern form as separate from religion. Critics believe that this integration and synthesis misrepresents and dilutes specific global shamanic, indigenous practices. I argue that the integration is necessary and quite valuable, because it makes the essentials of cross-cultural shamanic practices applicable and accessible for contemporary life here in the West. The essence of shamanism can be salvaged by gathering the most consistent commonalities across world cultures and highlighting these principles to better understand the mystery of soul life, to access our true nature, our soul.

While I initially studied with anthropologist Michael Harner in what he termed "core shamanism," I have since worked to integrate shamanistic methodology with both psychology and religious mysticism (believing this offers a contextual model that helps to ground us in both earth and sky realms). Harner has faced criticism for taking pieces of diverse shamanic teachings and simplistically minimizing them into a set of universal shamanic techniques. Appreciating the value of Harner's synthesized invention, I continue in that spirit of integration and synthesis. I do believe we can benefit from greater synthesis of diverse disciplines, specifically psychology, philosophy, and religious mysticism, fostering integral unification. My model takes shamanism as not only a religious phenomenon but a psychological, social, ethnic, philosophical, and even theological one; hence, an integral conceptualization is essential. The work of Eliade, who argued that the world's global shamanisms must have had a common source *as the original religion of humanity* (as early as the Paleolithic era), is central to my understanding. My working definition of this complex phenomenon of shamanism is that it is a technique of ecstasy, which is the communication of the Soul: a desired state of transcendent consciousness that can answer back to the stressful demands of today's modern world (as well as the stressful demands of a survival mentality of ancient pasts).

Born in Bucharest in 1907, Mircea Eliade was for many years the Sewell L. Avery Distinguished Service Professor of the History of Religions at the University of Chicago. His book on shamanism, *Archaic Techniques of Ecstasy*, was published in 1964 as part of Mythos: The Princeton/Bollingen Series in World Mythology, which formats many classic and influential studies on world mythology. Eliade's other books that also include discussion of shamanic principles are *The Myth of the Eternal Return* (1954) and *The Sacred and the Profane: The Nature of Religion* (1957). His groundbreaking works often discuss myth, symbol, and ritual—all central to shamanic practice. It is Eliade who identifies shamanism as a mysticism, and for this reason he distinguishes himself from many of today's anthropologists in the West. Many who write about shamanism (cross-culturally) generally agree that the shaman traverses the *axis mundi*, entering the Spirit World by effecting a transition of consciousness, entering into an ecstatic trance. The methods employed are diverse—depending on where you are in the world—and can be used together in an integrated fashion, incorporating practices from all around the globe to reach ecstatic, expanded states of consciousness. As we each reconnect with our soul individually and live connected to this expanded consciousness of Universal Soul, we then have greater potential to create and sustain soulful societies as each individual brings both body and soul into good and right humanitarian action.

In Western culture today, shamanism (as revealed mostly through the lens of anthropologists) is not thought of so much as a religion but as a technique for altering consciousness and a form of psychological and spiritual self-help. Viewed through a theological/mystical/psychological lens, this practice can help us clear negative imprints in the energy field before they are expressed as disease in the body (known as extraction practice), can cure "soul loss" and foster embodied soul retrieval, and can recover our vitality and life purpose, helping the practitioner maintain vibrant spiritual, mental, and physical health as a unified whole.

Shamanic practice teaches that invisible dimensions are layered upon our world and that many paranormal or mystical experiences occur when there are openings between the physical (earth) and the spiritual (sky) worlds. It is the shaman's calling to lift the veil and commune with the rocks, the trees, the plants, the elements (earth, water, fire, air, ether), and all the soul helpers to retrieve lost and disowned aspects of the self and the soul, both for the individual and for the community. For those of us who have little to no experience with shamanism, we can still recognize when these doorways, or portals, often open at unexpected times. For example, when one witnesses the passing of a loved one or endures an incredibly debilitating loss, often some sort of message or insight will calm and enlighten. When we experience the death of a loved one, for example, it becomes so clear that the energy that once was, is no longer within the physical vessel of the body. However, it seems unfathomable, almost impossible, that this energy could simply disappear. In confronting death, the living are left to ponder the existential questions of life: Where does this energy now exist? Can I dialogue with this energy in a realm other than where I now am? Is there some aspect of me that knows something I am not allowing myself to fully know?

Shamanism is now part of Western culture, thanks to Michael Harner, the anthropologist responsible for the formulation of core shamanism here in the West. Harner drew his key ideas from the remarkable similarities in the structure of "shamanic landscapes" as they were experienced by shamans from different cultures on opposite sides of the world, even separated by vast amounts of time. Alberto Villoldo, PhD, a medical anthropologist, believes that the shaman is the neuroscientist of enlightenment. He states that shamans perceive a luminous energy field enveloping the physical body that holds a record of all our past traumas and future possibilities.[4] Mircea Eliade describes how the shaman is the master of ecstasy and holds the knowledge of the techniques of religious ecstasy. In shamanic states of consciousness, time in the linear sense of past, present, and future becomes linked like a movie reel—with little to no separation. This is very much like the *ouroboros* symbol, which represents the idea of primordial unity, the belief in something existing from the beginning, with qualities that cannot be extinguished—also much like my working definition of the life of the soul.

Carl Jung, while drawing from a psychological model, said that the ouroboros has an archetypal significance to the human psyche—a meaning of infinity or wholeness.[5] From a shamanic perspective, the Soul Realm is not the realm of the imagination. It is an expanded state of consciousness, a sacred reality that can be accessed once one respects and understands the code to unlock its knowing. There are certain laws that govern this state of consciousness as a path of direct revelation. *These laws must be respected or the information will not be revealed.*

As Eliade states in his book *The Sacred and the Profane*, humans become aware of the sacred because it manifests itself as something wholly different from the profane. To designate the act of manifestation of the sacred, he proposes the term "hierophany." It is a fitting term, because it does not imply anything further; it expresses no more than what is implicit in its etymological content, i.e., that *something sacred shows itself to us*. It could be said that the history of religions—from the most primitive to the most highly developed—is constituted of a great number of hierophanies, manifestations of sacred realities. From the most elementary hierophany (e.g., manifestation of the sacred in some ordinary object, such as a stone or a tree) to the supreme hierophany (which, for a Christian, is the incarnation of God in Jesus Christ, or for a Hindu is the Buddha), there is no solution of continuity. In each case we are confronted by the same mysterious act—the manifestation of something of a wholly different order, a reality that does not belong to our world, in objects that are an integral part of our natural, "profane" world."[6]

When shamanism is practiced as a daily hierophany, it will offer you experience after experience of "true religion"—defined as "your soul being free to soar because you know the meaning of true liberation, through a connection with Infinity." This is in contrast to limiting religious dogma, which, unfortunately, often lives internally as an oppressive, dominating repressant. As you deepen in the power of this work, you will see that introjected authoritative others no longer confine and define your soul's knowing. Your soul (along with your soul's helpers and guides) begins to function as primary authority. Drawing from shamanic methodology, as you work with your own soul's ascension, you will learn to do your own divination work (communicating directly with sacred revelation). Interruptive mediation from external, dominative, authoritative powers will no longer be functional or useful, particularly from those authorities who may operate in repressive and constrictive ways. You will be able to use your abilities to access higher realms of your own soul's intelligence through direct revelation, clear in its timely medicine, as guidance for problem solving specific to your needs. The wise information you will receive will provide you with internal support, and, over time, as you become healthier and feel more whole you will realize that the information is trustworthy and authoritative in its own right. Much to their surprise and relief, many of my clients have been amazed at the durability of this healing work.

In this process of the soul's unraveling, ancient healing symbols join with the divine beings and soul guides who await our call, offering their mystical medicine. Magically, healing occurs as the cellular level is accessed, as well as the bones and the blood. Shamanism is associated with the belief called "animism," which is derived from the Latin word for soul, *anima*. Animists believe that everything in their world is alive and has a hidden aspect that can be seen only if a person allows for "seeing to be seen." Everything in the world—not just people, but animals, plants, trees, and rocks—has a soul or spirit that awaits our dialogue. We begin to imagine it is possible to learn to trust that these beings are authoritative and insightful, because our soul dialogues with them in an interactive manner and through these dialogues we receive meaningful guidance. We see that these beings are eager to reawaken in us a *belief* in a magical time when the portals of informational flow were open and we could pass easily between the visible and the invisible. This was a time before the veil was closed due to the wounded imprint. It is often the younger aspects of ourselves (ages five through nine) that are more trusting of this magico-mystical gnosis. This is why it is so important to retrieve these younger aspects of self through the psychological work of grounding in our bodies and learning to practice self-awareness and containment of our chronological bodymind selves.

CHAPTER 2
UNVEILING THE VEILED MYSTERIES

The Breeze at Dawn

The Breeze at Dawn has secrets to tell you.
Don't go back to sleep.
You must ask for what you really want.
Don't go back to sleep.
People are going back-n-forth across the door sill
Where the two worlds touch.
The door is Round and Open.
Don't go back to sleep.

Rumi

To practice shamanism is to have an understanding of the practical and experiential, yet ancient, indigenous wisdom accessible for contemporary life day after day. This can provide a ground for spiritual vision within an interfaith, multicultural perspective, which means that you can easily draw upon and integrate your particular faith tradition, if you have one (this is possible even with a pagan or pluralist tradition). Shamanism and soul journeying, while not requiring a particular religious worldview, can provide multiple experiences of soul retrieval and soul attachment. These are journeys and memorable experiences of direct revelation, through which the soul returns home to live permanently inside the body. *Once the body becomes a psychologically safe vessel, the soul will share its timeless secrets, offering guidance and wisdom.*

As described in Maslow's psychological model, the "hierarchy of needs," reaching the pinnacle of self-actualization must first be rooted in physiological safety. Once this is achieved, basic belonging is experienced, followed by love and evolutionary ascension. As we heal and grow, we are reconfigured as self-actualized beings, inviting an elevated morality, creativity, and problem-solving ability that radiates from the inner world to the outer whole. Inner evolutionary advancement creates revolutionary change. As we heal our interior, core wounding—*our detachment from our soul*—we will not only heal ourselves by reattaching with our very soul; we will have a greater interest, a vital energy, serving a just conscience and a greater refined awareness as well as unconditional love to offer the larger world, potentially leading to the creation of a soulful society.

Throughout the ages, many elder mystics and shamans in the differing disciplines of religion, philosophy, and spiritual mythology disseminated oral sacred knowledge to inquiring students. Those who showed themselves worthy of the secrets were chosen as initiates by the community and the elders. Within these sacred oral traditions were sacred listening practices teaching that specific guidelines must be followed in order for the student to "pass through the eye of the needle," to cross a certain revered threshold illuminated by many spiritual traditions. This mystical knowledge is passed on through the practices of these sacred spiritual traditions in an ecumenical manner, awakening an interfaith, multicultural perspective. Whether Native American spirituality, Celtic spirituality, shamanism, Sufism, Christian mysticism, or Yoga philosophies, to name a few, all similarly teach that once we pass through the portal, a veil will be lifted and the code unlocked. This is the unveiling of the Holy Mysteries.

In this crack of light, the Great Ones stitch while our soul sews; our destiny's tapestry unfolds one stitch at a time. It is not uncommon, while in a shamanic state, to see a needle and thread, as if things are being permanently sewn back together through the perspective of the soul's initial wholeness. As we learn to see into this hidden universe and trust what we see, our vision sees and our feet walk as the "magical flight" unfolds into clarity for next steps on this physical journey. Here, our soul's information is unraveled before us and we begin to understand and interpret the sacred secrets revealed—one step at a time, specific to the need of our soul's ascension for today. This needle and thread is a visual reminder of the integration of the varying disciplines. The word "tantra" is often used to describe this totality of the whole. Likewise, in Native American spiritual traditions, Grandmother Spider weaves the web of unity and interconnectedness. As you experience this needle and thread, know that the spirit weavers are weaving your web, moving you toward greater integration, unification, and healing. The inner ground of your being, once unified, can better support and sustain your soul within your body in a sanctified way. The durability of this work in the interiority of the self will have tremendous constructive ramifications in your outer world. The way in which you maneuver the complexities of the relationships in your life will be markedly different. You will begin to experience the rewards of an inner alignment as the attributes and characteristics of your rejuvenated soul enhance your life, a life now lived from your heart's center, from a core of unconditional love.

"God is not found in the soul by adding anything but by a process of subtraction," Christian mystic and theologian Meister Eckhart observed in the fourteenth century.[1] Eckhart, who wrote on metaphysics and spiritual psychology, observed that the unveiling and unraveling (what shamanism calls the "dismemberment") must occur in order to access that "tiny seed of memory" within. Shamanism refers to this process as the "release" and the "retrieval." Although you might expect that it would, religion, as a discipline of thought, has not been too helpful in teaching a clear methodology or providing a "how-to" manual on how to access the Soul Realm. The early Hebrews apparently debated a concept of the soul but did not separate it from the body, though later Jewish writers did further develop the idea of the soul. Biblical references to the soul are related to the concept of breath and establish no clear distinction between the ethereal soul and the corporeal body. Christian concepts of a body-soul dichotomy originated with the ancient Greeks and were introduced into Christian theology at an early date by St. Gregory of Nyssa (d. 394 C.E.) and by St. Augustine (d. 450 C.E.). Neither of these sources, while they are both provocative, provides the necessary how-to manual.

In understanding Christian theology historically, we can look back to St. Augustine, who spoke of the soul as a "rider" on the body, making clear the dualistic split between the material and the immaterial, *with emphasis on the soul representing the "true" person*. Even though the body and soul were separate, it was not possible to conceive of a soul without its body. In the Middle Ages, St. Thomas Aquinas returned to the Greek philosophers' concept of *the soul as a motivating principle of the body,* again, independent yet requiring the substance of the body to make an individual. While this is a conceptually useful debate, I ask again, where is my how-to manual? How do I experience my own soul with some sort of certainty, so that I might have more phenomenological evidence?

In Western philosophy, from the Middle Ages onward, the existence and nature of the soul and its relationship to the body continued to be disputed. To René Descartes, the human being was a union of the body and the soul, each a distinct substance acting on the other. The soul was equivalent to the mind. To Benedict de Spinoza, body and soul formed two aspects of a single reality. Immanuel Kant concluded that the soul was not demonstrable through reason, although the mind inevitably must reach the conclusion that the soul exists, because such a conclusion was necessary for the development of ethics and religion. To William James, at the beginning of the twentieth century, the soul as such did not exist at all but was merely a collection of psychic phenomena.

Just as there have been wide debates about the relationship of the soul to the body, there have been numerous ideas about when the soul comes into existence, and when and whether it dies. Ancient Greek beliefs were varied and evolved over time. Pythagoras, the Greek philosopher, mathematician, and mystic, who lived in the late sixth century BCE, held that the soul was of divine origin and existed before and after death. Plato and Socrates also accepted the immortality of the soul, while Aristotle considered only part of the soul, the *noûs*, or intellect, to have that quality. Early Christian philosophers adopted the Greek concept of the soul's immortality and thought of the soul as being created by God and infused into the body at conception. While this is all interesting to ponder and curious to reflect upon, something is terribly lacking in these soul theories. Phenomenological truth, the subjective structure of experience altering consciousness, is not discussed much in these circles of debate.

It is primarily through my practice of shamanism—and more recently through my study of yogic philosophy—that I feel as though I am just beginning to "get it"; and no sooner do I feel this than I cycle back into "I don't get it at all." Believing oneself to be a novice (which you may experience as well) indicates that one is in the glorious realm of Mystery. Each of us is subjectively awakened to a different understanding of the varied ways of accessing our own soul, meaning that certain paths call to us individually while others don't. Paths like shamanism, yoga, and Hinduism each offer an embodied methodology. There is great value in the somatic psychologies, which educate people in being grounded first in the body before launching off into the world of Spirit. Shamanism's pathway inward is through the drumbeat, mimicking the heartbeat, awakening the chambers of the heart to open more deeply to universal unconditional love. As we learn to merge with the Soul Realm and understand the interrelatedness of the visible and the invisible, the physical and the spiritual, the form and the formless, we merge our humanity with our divinity, experiencing ourselves as whole beings.

Yoga, one embodied soulful path, emphasizes the *atman*—"breath," or "soul." Both shamanism and Yoga acknowledge the Soul as the universal, eternal self of which each individual soul (*jiva* or *jiva-atman*) partakes. In Hinduism, the jiva-atman is believed to be eternal and is imprisoned in an earthly body at birth. Hindus believe that at death the jiva-atman passes into a new existence determined by karma, or the cumulative consequences of actions. The cycle of death and rebirth (*samsara*) is eternal according to some Hindus, but others say it persists only until the soul has attained karmic perfection, thus merging with the Absolute (Brahman, another term for Soul Realm). Perhaps it is through the yoga practice, the daily practice of honoring the breath in the body, that the Hindus became enlightened in their understanding about the soul. One has to wonder, according to the great Yogatattva Upanishad, "Without the practice of yoga, how could knowledge set the soul free?"[2] For it is through "the cessation of the agitation of the mind" (yoga defined) that we learn to access these other aspects of our consciousness.

In shamanism there is the notion that the soul fragments from the body in times of trauma, abuse, chronic adversity, or lack of psychological safety. As a result, the soul needs to be retrieved, in effect called home, and fortunately there are helpers for this process. Through shamanism, yoga, and the natural world, we can find a more deeply embodied experience of union with the Divine, the hidden, unseen realm of transcendence. This experience is what I mean by the term "embodied enlightenment." Many yoga poses are the embodiment of the divine beings and spirit helpers who appear in shamanic states of consciousness to offer their medicine. As we practice embodying a pose, we can imagine the essence, or medicine, of the animal or entity for whom that pose is named imparting its healing energies to us. For example, eagle pose, crow pose, cobra (the serpent of transmutation) pose, dolphin pose, turtle pose, cow pose, sun salutations, and moon poses each in their own way remind us that it is in these bodies that we are paying homage to both earth and sky as well as everything in between. This physical balancing act is required for our soul to return home, at peace in the body; this peace is what we experience as we move into the final pose of a yoga session: *savasana*, death pose.

It is understandable that there is so much crossover and overlap between shamanism and yoga, two enduring ancient, global practices. Both bow in homage to sun and moon alignment, invoking balance, in the internal body, between feminine powers (moon energies) and masculine powers (the sun's rays). As we go more deeply into our physical bodies and find balance between the polarities of giving and receiving, we begin to experience ourselves at peace in our own skin and learn to die to that which is no longer needed. Wholeness and integration become a real experience, not just a concept discussed intellectually, as we practice release and retrieval through each breath. As we commune comfortably with both our inner sun and inner moon energies, before we know it, we will be brought home to our true nature, our soul. Even Carl Jung, the psychiatrist who introduced Eastern spiritual disciplines to the West, wrote about a moon consciousness symbolic of the circle of our soul's past/present/future consciousness. There is something about the roundness of the frame drum that meets the roundness of the moon and the roundness of the sun to bring us home to the circle of our soul's consciousness, merging with an expansive interconnectedness.

Moon and Sun Energies Explained

Just as the sun is the center of our solar system, when we work with the sun in shamanic states of consciousness, its penetrating rays will affect our solar plexus, our center, with its golden brilliance of red, orange, and yellow. Clarity, strength of will, and power to act in our own truth and integrity will be reignited as the root, sacral, and solar plexus chakras are recharged and realigned. But these energies by themselves leave us imbalanced as an organism. We need the energies of the moon that shines, because it reflects the light from the sun. These reflective energies of the feminine consciousness allow us to receive lightness of being and reflect it out into the world. As we learn to balance both sun and moon energies in these physical bodies, we feel connected to our willful strength and the power to act with clarity, as well as the tenderness, softness, vulnerability, and openness of a loving heart.

Feminine energies are different from the energies of the sun. Moon consciousness reminds us to stay open and receptive to that which is waiting to reveal itself to us. We are given eyes to see in the midst of the darkness as light is reflected to us and through us. Just as the moon shines in the darkness of the midnight sky, moon consciousness illuminates the hidden realms of the unseen universe. This intertwined relationship of sun and moon consciousness mirrors the dance of shared powers and reveals the need for masculine and feminine energies to be in constructive interaction, with a shared balance of power between them. This is in stark contrast to an inner power struggle of opposing forces, typically described in psychological terms as "intrapsychic conflict." The path the earth takes around the sun is elliptical, meaning the sun and the moon waver and morph between close and far apart, again mirroring the fluidity of movement between contact and withdrawal, moving toward and moving away, always seeking that beautiful union of harmony and balance. Honoring the characteristic differences of these seemingly polarized energies in our internal body (while containing and integrating their healing medicine) will foster an external world of greater nonviolence, harmony, and wholeness. The healing symbol of Infinity (internally applied) will bring us home to a natural balance on a regular basis, if we allow it. From an inner world of peace and an open heart full of unconditional loving, the global world will begin to shift, one community at a time. Intrapsychic harmony leads to interpersonal peace.

In my shamanic psychotherapeutic work with the healing energy of the goddess Isis, the symbol atop her head is related to sun and moon consciousness unified, facing the upper, expansive world of Spirit. Many different theories exist about the specific meaning of this imagery, most (men) agreeing that this symbol is about a sun consciousness. However, this has not been my phenomenological experience in my dialogue with Isis and my practical application of its work with my clients. Again, working with the ancient healing symbols and the different beings of the Soul Realm will provide you with the information you need specific to the medicine offered: you don't have to take my word for it (and your direct phenomenological revelation may be different from what you will read in this book). Understand that this can get tricky as soul helpers morph and shape-shift, often drawing upon multiple meanings and interpretations; remaining open to this play is key, and repeatedly asking the Soul Realm for clarity and assurance always helps. A symbol may hold a different significance for you than it does for another. This is why we need to remember that we are in the realm of Holy Mystery whenever we begin to experience ourselves becoming too fundamentalist or dogmatic about the specifics of the ultimate "answer." The fruitful tension of holding both the knowing of gnosis revealed and the not-knowing of the Holy Mystery is essential. When we listen carefully from the essence of our core being, we know when we are in the presence of that which is both fruitfully and fulfillingly meaningful to our own soul.

LIFTING THE VEIL

The metaphor of the unknown cave of our soul beckons to each one of us, confirming our longing to be known and pursued by calling us inward so that we can more accurately interpret the circumstances of our lives. As a client recently said to me, "Going inside to discover my true nature appears to be the *only* pathway *in*." How true. The Soul Realm responds generously to those who seek, bestowing gifts of inner vision, clarity, and wisdom to those who believe and exhibit "eyes to see and ears to hear."

The power of the moon in expanding human consciousness is believed to be magnetic. Carl Jung wrote of the "moon-like consciousness" as a way of seeing in which we more readily perceive oneness rather than bifurcation or dualistic differentiation. As we learn to deepen into this moon-like consciousness (which will organically happen as you apply the principles of this book to your daily life) we begin to resonate rhythmically with the cycles of the moon and we understand the continuity of the cycles of life, relating intuitively. We learn to invite feminine wisdom to live more present in our consciousness, allowing our actions and minds to be informed by a different internal knowing. Much as the moon moves the sea, it has moved us into many a mystical moment. This deepening into the Soul Realm, with its varying aspects of consciousness, can be a leap of faith into the arms of Great Mystery, where we learn to trust the information of our souls, allowing ourselves to be remembered and reconfigured.

ILLNESS AS A WAKE-UP CALL

Messages, as if from death's wise voice, keep coming to me. While I write this book, the awareness of death surrounds me. I am keenly aware of the way in which many of our dreams die and how we struggle to hold onto life. Not just the physical reality of death, but the way in which we live with dying every day yet don't often name the experience as death. We lose husbands, wives, jobs, and houses. Marriage ends in divorce. Friends betray our trust and rock our feeling of safety in the world. Children leave home for college and we somehow adapt to an empty nest. Part of what it means to keep choosing life is to learn how to re-create ourselves after the loss of that which is very dear to us. The Soul Realm is intimately acquainted with the birth/life/death/rebirth cycle and can better teach us to revere this process of letting go, exercising the "bounce-back technique."

I've experienced this wake-up call most acutely when my husband was diagnosed with an auto-immune illness that required him to receive chemotherapy for several years. When I went with him for his treatments at the cancer ward of the hospital, the experience of the struggle for life and the way in which life and death lay side by side was undeniable. As I lay by his side, I recognized the familiar smells I used to absorb while interning as a chaplain, working with hospice. I found myself studying the faces around me, contemplating death among the living, noticing the way in which the "living dead" appear to be soulless. For days afterward, I felt as though I was all used up, like a sack of sludge waiting to be emptied. I knew that my body, with its semipermeable boundaries, had absorbed the fear, the worry, and the terror that surround death.

The soul recognizes life and death as one. It is our soul that intimately understands that the life/death/rebirth cycle is intrinsic to nature. Our souls are not afraid of death but recognize it as a natural part of the whole of life. The soul innately understands that death brings life. Hinduism offers distinctions for this triune force as Brahma, the Creator; Vishnu, the Preserver; and Shiva, the Destroyer. We see these life/death/rebirth cycles in the seasons of nature: spring, summer, fall, winter. Just as the daffodils and tulips pop up from the seemingly dead earth to create such beauty after the harshness of winter, embedded in the very nature of the soul is the recognition that in dying, we live. The soul does not fear death, change, or the mini-death experiences of shedding old skins. I am speaking not only about the finality of the death experience when we leave this material plane, but also about the many smaller deaths we experience in living our lives. Somewhere inside we carry the knowledge that our souls do not revere fear. In fact, it is often those things we fear the most, *that we try the most to avoid*, that are deeply reflective of and congruent with our soul's hidden purpose, which is seeking revelation.

LETTING GO

And he said, Naked I came from my mother's womb, And naked I shall return there. The Lord gave and the Lord has taken away. Blessed be the name of the Lord.

JOB 1:21

Because the Soul Realm is intimately acquainted with this birth/life/death/rebirth cycle, it respects change as inevitable, even necessary, for our own soul's evolutionary development. There is a core appreciation that the letting-go, "death-layer process" is essential in order to expand. As mentioned earlier, in shamanic methodology this is referred to as release-and-retrieval. Embodied in this way of life is a basic acceptance of the repetitive process of change and the necessity of letting go—ceasing to hoard in the container of the body—in order to be reconfigured into newfound freedom, inner spaciousness, and lightness of being. In order for us to be reborn into newly evolved spirit beings, we learn to release, die to, or exhale that which must go. This release often includes the shattering of our wounded personalities and the dissolution of our comfort zones. You may experience this process as a quiet trembling similar to the tremors after a good orgasm. This similar state is experienced in savasana or shamanic states of consciousness when one is being reconfigured and the release is occurring. Allow yourself to surrender to this process as you open to the ancient knowing of who you truly are.

As a client I'll call George exclaimed after a shamanic journeying session, "Wow! I cannot believe how my inner body feels so spacious. And I can hear my mind saying to me, *Come on George! You sound crazy. What are you talking about?* But I have to listen to my inside truth, because I know what I am feeling now and it is simply an internal spaciousness that has returned hope to my being." George was observing what most clients experience when the work is complete. The clearing has taken place and they discover in the interior cavity of the body a new-found fertility—waiting to be birthed into new life, an expanded consciousness.

While one is in shamanic states of consciousness, it is common to be met by the Angel of Death, the one called Azra'il in the Sufi tradition. This is the being from the upper world who oversees the transition from death to resurrection. This can occur with the many smaller deaths we die in a lifetime. Hank Wesselman refers to this being as "the Threshold Guardian"[3] and Joseph Campbell, "the power that watches at the threshold to the unknown."[4] This Angel of Death is deeply invested in shaking and shattering our perceived grip on reality—the clutching fist we exercise often apart from awareness—and loosening the attachments to what we think we know to be true about our life's plan. In my shamanic experience, the Angel of Death consistently shows up in a black cape, very discernible, leaning against the side of a triangular corner or wall, arms crossed at the solar plexus. This being appears at the intersection where one wall meets another, forming a pinnacle like a triangle, reminding us that he lives in the cross-section where the two worlds meet. There this Angel of Death stands beneath his caped veil, not saying a word but supporting the transitional passage through the portal. When I explained to my Sufi friend this appearance, she confirmed, "Oh, yes, that is Azra'il. He appears to me looking identical to your description."

When I am working with clients who are moving into their soul's emergence while facing death-layer experiences (metaphorically speaking), this Angel of Death often appears, reassuring them that the death/rebirth preparatory work has been completed. This revelation builds trust and support for the emergence into ascension of soul. When the Angel of Death appears, it confirms that the unknown of the fertile void is present among us and can be trusted. This visitation ritualistically marks a significant death/rebirth rite of passage and sears it into our consciousness. Again, this being is quite different from other beings in the Soul Realm who lure us into the cave of the unknown. Each ascended being appears to have a distinct purpose as they oversee the soul's passage into heightened ascension; it is important that you learn to dialogue with each spirit being to understand for yourself with clarity.

An animal spirit, such as that of a deer, may emerge to lure us into the unknown of the woods for a new adventure, showing us the many thresholds and passages that it will be necessary for us to enter in order to move through a transitional state into greater expansion and self-expression of soul. The appearance of the Angel of Death, however, is testimony to a critical juncture of ending sandwiched side by side with a new beginning. This angel's presence signifies the important ritual of death and dying in life, promising resurrection into greater soul retrieval and new life unfolding. The greater my experience trusting this work, the more I see consistency in the essence of each spirit being's purpose—similar to the concept that each soul has a unique purpose, so too, does each being in the Soul Realm. Even after sixteen years, I am still a student in this inquiry. The fact that this practice is a phenomenological experience of direct inquiry and direct revelation only reinforces that we are in a face-to-face encounter in the metaphysical world, to dialogue with each spiritual being in order to understand its medicine more specifically. Each spirit helper and divine being has a specific essence, or medicine, for a specific need. Our job is to receive, to dialogue, to trust—just as we do in the intimate relationships of this material, physical world. Be brave and say, "Hello. Are you my teacher? What is the medicine you have for me today?"

It is very important that you take the leap to engage, even argue and wrestle, with these different beings from the Soul Realm. With time, you will begin to understand what each being's medicine is about. If not, ask for more information and greater clarity. Our souls want us to always remember to listen to their wisdom as they offer us messages, truths, and reflections from their otherworldly perspective. Our human challenge is to not minimize or dismiss the information as it passes through.

Recently, while working with me in shamanic session, Bill experienced a visitation from frog medicine, and then the frog jumped down his throat (which of course Bill found repulsive). The frog dialogued with him, reminding him of his metamorphosis to come. Having just turned fifty and pursuing a new career path, Bill was told that the frog was a symbol of his coming into his own creative powers (which he had forgotten about). As the frog focused in on just "the eye of the frog," piercing Bill's awareness and entire being, Bill found himself awakening to see and understand, in his third eye of inner vision, that significant change would be unfolding and that he would not be doing what he thought he was "supposed to do" with his life. Having lived his life by "shoulds" and "supposed tos," he found this both comforting and scary. Frog let Bill know that he would be his power animal for this time of transition and help him leap into new climatic conditions, no longer mired in the mud of the mundaneness of life. Like the content that unveiled itself through this shamanic session, our souls have valuable information to share with us so that we can be empowered to live our days with strength, courage, authenticity, and vulnerability, better capable of navigating life's challenges.

My hope is that, as you read this book, you will quicken your awareness of your soul's imagery and language so that you can become a better interpreter of its voice and your body can become and remain a safe container for your soul. Even if Leapfrog appears to you, allow yourself to be guided by this beautiful spirit. It will be medicine specific to your soul's need, encouraging you to take that leap of faith into greater soul configuration.

Accessing the Soul Realm can also be harnessed as a simple tool for relaxing into the presence of all that is and creating a brief respite from a stressful day. In the psychological community, we call this "mindfulness," or the practice of "compassionate presence." As you practice the suggestions in the book, you will find yourself better able to calm overwhelming or fluctuating emotional states, and you will naturally develop daily self-nourishing practices that will feed a deepened self-love and self-acceptance. You will find that, as your confidence grows and you experience greater mastery and autonomy with self-management, you'll notice that you are less reactive and more creative.

As you deliberately sustain a sacred space for yourself in the temple/container of your own body, you will deepen into a peaceful state of ease while you wait with anticipation to see what or who unfolds as your soul's guides in the unseen universe. Over time and with consistency of practice, you will discover that the material in this book will awaken your curiosity and arouse your receptivity, so that you will want to inquire more determinedly about your own soul. You will learn through this practice to harness your soul's power for daily strength, clarity of action, and powerful purpose, manifesting your fullness more expansively in the world. Remember Mircea Eliade's words about sacred space, keeping in mind my notion of your body as a constant, sacred space of holding, as "Holy Temple":

> The man of the archaic societies tends to live as much as possible in the sacred or in close proximity to consecrated objects. The tendency is perfectly understandable, because, for primitives as for the man of all pre-modern societies, the sacred is equivalent to a power, and, in the last analysis, to reality. The sacred is saturated with being. Sacred power means reality and at the same time enduringness and efficacy. The polarity sacred-profane is often expressed as an opposition between real and unreal or pseudo-real. Thus it is easy to understand that religious man deeply desires to be, to participate in reality, to be saturated with power.[5]

CHAPTER 3
GATEWAY TO THE UNSEEN UNIVERSE

Inside myself is a place where I live alone
and that's where I renew my springs that never dry up.

PEARL S. BUCK

"Soul" has been a widely debated concept in a variety of disciplines throughout the ages. Is it possible that each of us could know, with certainty, that we inhabit a soul in the same way in which we are certain that we inhabit our bodies? And, if so, how would we even begin to conceive of our own soul? Drawing from the field of philosophy, soul is viewed as the immaterial aspect or essence of a human being that somehow mysteriously confers both individuality and humanity. In theology, the soul is defined as that part of the individual that partakes of divinity; it is often considered to survive the death of the body. For centuries, many indigenous cultures with practicing communal shamans have recognized incorporeal principles of human existence corresponding to the immortal spiritual soul. There is evidence, even among prehistoric peoples, of a belief in an aspect distinct from the body yet residing in it. What we see from these differing perspectives is that any discussion about the soul certainly encompasses paradox, mystery, and maybe even, upon extended exploration, greater complexity.

Perhaps this conversation about mystery initially raises more questions than fundamentally definitive answers. To that, I say, "Good. Job well done." Learning to respect and revere the land of mystery means understanding that sometimes there lies greater wisdom in the questions than in the answers. Even the field of psychology offers minimal methodology or discussion about the soul's relevance for psychotherapy. It wasn't until my initiation into shamanic methodology that I was awakened to a comprehensive framework and practical manual for further study and experience of the soul. With this practice, I learned how to retrieve a lost soul, given that the soul so easily fragments off from the body in times of trauma and survival threats. According to shamanic teaching, any early childhood trauma or even trauma experienced in the womb can be severe enough to cause the detachment of the soul from the haven of the body. In order to reveal itself to the body's inhabitant, the soul needs the container of the body to be psychologically safe; otherwise, it will not make its home in the physical body. The soul will splinter off and live in other realms of the unseen universe.

Ancient philosophical theories of soul were carefully conceptualized and widely debated by Plato, Aristotle, Epicurus, and the Stoics. Philosophic discussions address the soul but offer such divergence of thought that they often become more theoretical and less experiential. The ancient Greek concepts of the soul vary considerably according to the particular era and philosophical school and are, again, not very experiential or practical.

The Epicureans considered the soul, like the rest of the body, to be made up of atoms. For the Platonists, the soul was an immaterial and incorporeal substance, akin to the gods yet part of the world of change and becoming. Aristotle's concept of the soul was obscure, though he did express the opinion that it was a form inseparable from the body. Then there are the succinct statements, like the one from Herodotus, the fifth-century ancient Greek historian, who affirmed that "the destiny of man is in his own soul." For Pythagoras and Plato (and for all the varied mystery religions of the Greco-Roman world in the first four centuries BCE and beyond—not to mention the core of nearly all Paganism), the ancient wisdom texts focus on the miracle of divinity being embodied within human form. As Tom Harpur observes in *The Pagan Christ*:

> ...and this is of tremendous significance, the thoroughgoing studies of ancient religions done over many years by the scholars who have established with certainty that incarnation—the indwelling of God or divine essence in the human, every human—is the central teaching of all ancient belief systems everywhere.

Plato's ideas have been the most helpful in my work integrating psychology with shamanism. Platonic philosophy confirms that the soul's personality is intentional, in that its mission in the world is to fulfill its destiny. Each soul has a specific calling and it is this calling, or destiny (to use Plato's term), that preoccupies the soul's energies. The mission of the soul of each individual person ties into the mission of the collective pulse of the unseen universe. There is order and intentional direction to that which the Soul Realm wishes the soul to accomplish. This driving message does not go away and cannot be silenced without serious repercussions.[1]

THE RIVER OF FORGETFULNESS

The River of Life (as an ancient symbol in mythology and lore) represents the gentle push, or movement forward, from *the purifying water element*. This is a reminder that *our soul is interested in its ascension*, always cleansing and purifying, pulsating into greater ease and clarity, toward transparency and actualization. This crystallizes the characteristics of authenticity and vulnerability and helps us loosen and release the grip of shame. As someone once said to me, as he was moving forward through a difficult transition, "It's as though I have a river behind my ass." This becomes the visual reminder—if we allow ourselves to see it—that, daily, we are being carried by this River of Life even throughout all the earthly trials and challenges. The medicine of this water element teaches us to be flexible, shifting and turning with the necessary adaptations. This river also reminds us that the passage of time intrinsically carries a certain flow, or fluidity, throughout our soul's lifetime. This is why myth plays such an important role in the imagery of soul life; as we will continue to see, the way in which reality comes into existence is revealed by what is narrated in myth. The water element—considered holy in many sacred traditions—has a part in the re-membering of our soul's knowing. This calls in purity.

As we become more configured in the symbolism of our soul, our purification is the result, removing that which must go to make way for the new. The water element, when functioning as medicine, may also show itself as a waterfall caressing the crown of your head or perhaps as the sea swirling inside and around you. Throughout the shamanic journey, water will morph into its many different forms, teaching you that you, too, can practice morphing with the vibration of life. When you see this water element, be sure to awaken intentionally to its powerful medicine, remembering that the River of Life is always the force answering back to the River of Forgetfulness.

The River of Forgetfulness is an experience none of us escape. The name alone captures a distinct eeriness, sending a shiver up our spine. Somewhere, perhaps way back, we really do remember this immersion into a dark baptism. In the Myth of Er, at the end of Plato's *Republic*, Plato tells of the empty arrival into this world due to the River of Forgetfulness. Not only do we humans forget our past incarnations but we also forget our divine origin upon being birthed. Theologians, philosophers, and psychological theorists known for their existential and phenomenological explorations of the question of Being have referred to this as the "concealment of Being," or "forgetting of Being," or "loss of true nature." *This detachment of soul from the body necessitates the pursuit that defines our central nature.* Because we forget what we know, we need to be awakened to this unforgetfulness, also referred to as "awakening into consciousness." This "unconcealment" has many different names in various disciplines, yet we all know when we are having this experience.

Spiritual traditions and the Celtic shamans refer to this process as "the lifting of the veil." In Celtic mythology, it is the Lady of the Lake who determinedly assists in lifting this veil, bringing about the transition from unseeing to seeing. In this physical plane, walking the edge of the sands of the beaches, where the shore meets the sea or where the river meets the bank, is the symbolism for visiting these sacred sites (sights)—where the two worlds merge and there is, but there isn't, a mysterious union where the two become one. The medicinal elements and the ancient symbols from nature appear while the veil lifts; we see with more clarity into the constancy of the unseen universe in these archetypal moments. William Wordsworth captures this in his "Ode: Intimations of Immortality":

> Our birth is but a sleep and a forgetting:
> The Soul that rises with us, our life's Star,
> Hath had elsewhere its setting,
> And cometh from afar:
> Not in entire forgetfulness,
> And not in utter nakedness,
> But trailing clouds of glory do we come
> From God, who is our home.[2]

A Seed of Memory

The seed of God is in us. If you are an intelligent and hard-working farmer, it will thrive and grow up into God, whose seed it is, and its fruits will be God-fruits, pear seeds grow into pear trees, nut seeds grow into nut trees, and God seeds grow into God.

Meister Eckhart

Significantly, Meister Eckhart, a German Dominican mystic who died before he could be fully tried for heresy by the Archbishop of Cologne, once wrote that the Christ was not a historical person, per se, but rather "the collective soul of humanity," the reflection of the light, the "sun God." It appears as though the primary truth of human culture presented by all sage religions of antiquity is that there resides deeply embedded in the core of our basic constitution a nucleus of this Christ, a divine spark, or sun, that rises and sets daily.[3]

The River of Life Is a Fluid, Transformative, Healing Force

Religions across many cultures embrace different symbols, whose surface meaning appears to be only a veneer potentially masking their deeper, essential truth. A mystical river, the River of Life, whose waters cleanse and purify and bring a calming balm to its bathers, appears repetitively in many different sacred literatures of the ancient world. This River of Life also appears repeatedly in healing work, affirming the transformative powers of the purifying medicine of the water element. The storytelling from the sacred mystical traditions teaches that those who drink from this river remember everything and even attain omniscience. Initiates were taught that they would be offered aid, magical wisdom, and a restoration of personal power and balance if they chose to drink from its waters.

Each of us carries a tiny seed of memory about the restorative powers of this River somewhere in our fiber. The invitation, to us as humans, is to either nurture or neglect this seed of information—to either re-member or re-press the River's reemergence of our awakening into conscious knowledge. The River of Life seeks to talk back to the River of Forgetfulness; allow them to dialogue internally and travel with full, flowing authenticity, waking up the sleeping state.

The unseen, *constant* universe is available and eager to share its secrets with us. Wise guidance and sacred knowledge from other realms of consciousness are ours to embrace. Learning how to listen to this voice is both a discipline and a skill that we can develop. Whether we call it God, Higher Self, Spirit, Higher Power, Source, or Soul, learning how to listen and remain open with both our hearts and our minds is central to this process of remembering what we believe we have forgotten. As we exercise this discipline and grow in knowledge, we build the knowing and the trust that our soul's evolutionary purpose will be fulfilled. To know the truth and to be set free is possible, not just words unintentionally expressed by Jesus. In his day, there were many sacred oral traditions still in existence, practiced by members who understood the metaphors from which Jesus spoke. To be born again is about our soul's reentering of this River of Forgetfulness while retrieving and remembering what we think we have forgotten.

Plato discussed the notion that each of us enters the world with a soul's destiny—what I refer to as the "soul's calling." Before our soul comes into our body at birth, it is believed that it exists elsewhere. "Where" is the subject matter of great theological and philosophical debate, which is beyond the scope of this text; however, through the practice of shamanism, we understand that the soul is that aspect of ourselves which is primordial and pure and timeless. Therefore, the soul cannot maintain its ease of habitat in a toxic, traumatized, or addicted body. If the body and mind are not in a state of health, wholeness, and receptivity, the soul will not be psychologically safe in the body, nor will it reveal its secrets. The soul's sole mission is to fulfill its destiny. The soul must feel safe in the container of the body to unveil itself.

CASE STUDY: HARRY'S EPIPHANY

Our souls are eager for us to distinguish between our woundedness and our soul's pure potentiality. Our souls intrinsically understand that the mysteries of life will be made available if we reach beyond our own self-limiting paradigms. Harry, one of my mid-life male clients, described the connection with his internal ten-year-old boy by saying, "I remember this experience of feeling so inadequate in my human body, yet I would look up at the sky and recognize my expansive nature and knew there was something more on the other side than all this pain and limitation." This is how it sounds when someone is trying to capture the soul's personality as gnosis, as a distinctly different entity from the wounded voice of the human personality's conditioning.

I have constructed an embodied conceptual model—which integrates Gestalt theory, shamanism, and elemental breath work—to help clarify and simplify these principles and root them in the body. This model works with the body as a container for embodiment, teaching first the necessity of grounding and rooting in this physical realm, which provides better management of both cognition and emotion in a psychologically safe way. Once the body practices self-management of cognition, thoughts, beliefs, and emotions, then the soul feels safe to come home and reside in the body while simultaneously remaining connected to the larger, cosmic Soul Realm. In various spiritual traditions it is understood that the soul leaves the body in times of trauma, abuse, grief, and loss—fragmenting off into some otherworldly sphere. As earthen vessels, when we psychologically embody in a safe and secure manner, we invite the soul back into the container of the body. The soul will then inform the body from the laws of a different universe. The soul's perception on any given circumstance will be markedly different from the human perspective.

Only when the body is a safe container will the soul come home and live fully expressed and unified with mind and emotion. Viewed from this contextual framework, the "divine personality," the soul, is a separate entity, or purer reality, separate from the woundedness of human personality (see figure on page 50 for further clarification). The work to be done is the integration of the two spheres in a manner that is rooted and grounded in the container of the body, holding the realm of matter while still expanded and open to the heavens, the Divine Realm.

As witness to countless moments of soul revelation within therapeutic sessions, I observe true nature, or authentic soul fully expressed, as a separate being from our personality, as we typically think of it. While the concept of "psyche" (soul) is imbedded in the crux of the word "psychology," there is actually very little about soul that is theorized in modern psychological modalities (other than Jungian psychology). Yet, time after time, I have been witness to the soul that emerges in the present moment as experienced by my clients. The soul insists that the body it resides in must wake up. This message has awakened in me a respectful curiosity to listen better in order to understand more, both for myself and for my clients.

> *The very thing which is now called the Christian religion existed among the ancients also, nor was it wanting from the inception of the human race until the coming of Christ in the flesh, at which point the true religion, which was already in existence, began to be called Christian.*[4]
>
> SAINT AUGUSTINE

SOUL PERSONALITY / THE INTENTIONAL SELF, VS. WOUNDED PERSONALITY / THE INTERRUPTED SELF

While growing up, many of us have been religiously, morally, or spiritually informed by our different faith traditions, but I would venture to guess that few of us have received a solid education about the specifics of soul retrieval. Many of you may have also had an experience with a psychotherapist—yet few therapists ever raise the question of soul within the therapeutic setting. What I am asking you to consider, using your critical faculties, is whether there may be an aspect of yourself that is more than the sum of your parts. Simply put, the breakdown of your being-ness could be body, mind, *and* soul, but your actual being-ness might just be your very soul: *mysteriously greater than the sum of mind and body and, in some mystical way, accessing a source of vision into a world that appears to be hidden.* Through the years of integrating shamanic healing methods within the psychotherapeutic session, I have witnessed individual souls partaking, even bathing, in the larger Soul Realm. Somehow we can magically and mysteriously plug in to something far greater than ourselves when we open our minds to this deeper reality.

The 12-Step programs refer to this sourcing as one's "Higher Power," which is simpatico with my language of Soul Realm. I see the soul having its own "personality," distinct from the human personality—which is replete with its finite limitations imprinted by the surrounding wounding environments. As we develop a practice of compassionate observational awareness—as opposed to judgmental triggered reactivity—we learn to observe the automatic nature of our wounded personality, more from a place of storytelling. Our narrative about ourselves voices our beliefs in our limitations and fears. The reactive habitual patterns of stuck behaviors work to reinforce our attachment to these beliefs as "true." Our soul, however, wants to awaken us to a different reality: the notion that we can speak and live a new story, creating new behaviors based on our true nature and not the narrative that we have been taught to believe about who we are.

Being in the presence of souls as they unravel is like watching a luscious pink rose bloom into its flowering expansiveness—or a peacock, greeting you on a wooded path, that spreads its thousand-eyed, iridescent, blue-green plumage, showing you something magnificent. The beauty of the purity of the soul is breathtaking as it allows itself to be seen in its disarming nakedness. Often, when I am in therapeutic sessions with clients, I am repeatedly struck by the two worldviews (psychological/physical and spiritual) while the two simultaneous realities unfold right before my eyes. Learning to hold both has taken years. The human personality of my client is steeped in all its conditioning, expressing the universality of the human struggle. Yet visual images of my clients' souls and messages from the Soul Realm dance around the room, talking to me, often in great contrast to what the client is saying from the imprint of the narrative of their wounded personality. Learning to hold this duality of perception, while understanding that the two views need not be incongruent, is essential. A conceptual model that mutually supports and holds both soul reality and wounded human experience allows the two worlds to dialogue internally and acquaint themselves (eventually peacefully) with each other. This illustration is my conceptual model, which can become a "quick tip" for living daily in embodied enlightenment as the soul re-parents the wounded imprint, gently reminding that a "mistaken identity" perception is flawed given its attachment to distortion.

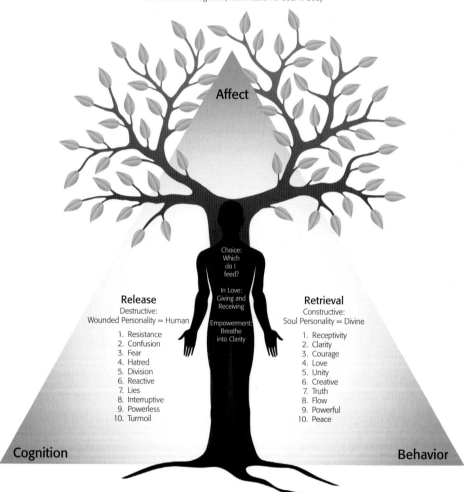

Enlightenment:
Live in Wisdom, Light and Love. Dialoguing Inside with Holy Mystery.

"Tri" Δ + Infinity of Movement ∞ (N⟷S, E⟷W) = O
Human Divine Integration, Reunification of Soul in Body

Affect

Choice:
Which
do I
feed?

In Love:
Giving and
Receiving

Empowerment:
Breathe
into Clarity

Release
Destructive:
Wounded Personality = Human

1. Resistance
2. Confusion
3. Fear
4. Hatred
5. Division
6. Reactive
7. Lies
8. Interruptive
9. Powerless
10. Turmoil

Retrieval
Constructive:
Soul Personality = Divine

1. Receptivity
2. Clarity
3. Courage
4. Love
5. Unity
6. Creative
7. Truth
8. Flow
9. Powerful
10. Peace

Cognition

Behavior

Embodiment: Walk in Congruence and Alignment

Unfortunately, the wounded personality believes the *lies* and *limitations* from our limited self, with its wounded imprint rooted in distortion. Our wounded personality is invested in the familiarity of the lies from the wounding environments and comfortably remains attached to those limitations. Our divine personality, our soul, also referred to as the "I Am" self, on the other hand, is expansive and unified with Infinity, the Eternal. Our soul's self-perception comes through the eyes of the Beloved adoringly gazing into our deeper truth of being-ness.

The diagram on page 50 represents the core mantra of this book (which we can practice so easily, daily, because our bodies are always with us): Embodiment in the root—enlightenment at the crown—empowerment in our solar plexus, the place of the will—love in our heart center. The core teaching of this embodied diagram is this:

We are embodied (root chakra) to be enlightened (crown chakra), to be empowered (solar plexus) in love (heart chakra). Which do I feed (throat chakra)? My wounded personality (right arm/hand)? Or my soul personality (left arm/hand placed over heart)? Our physical bodies become the opportunity for daily reminder of who we are in our soul.

Often, in my therapeutic work with clients, I will create an experiment, to awaken their awareness to the visceral feel of holding the two worlds (physical/spiritual) while embodied consciously in their body. The voice of the wounded personality insists on being heard, understood, and validated in its experience of growing up human in this world (as it should). However, often the wounded personality is masking its fear of change by remaining attached to the pain and suffering of the past's enduring themes. The wounded imprint of our lives repeats itself in patterns for so long that we begin to believe that the limited self is who we truly are. These debilitating patterns often become what we call "me," "my life," "the truth of who I am." What we don't always realize is that our soul is peering into our human experience, trying to offer us a different lens through which to see ourselves and our lives.

THE GUEST HOUSE

This being human is a guest house.
Every morning a new arrival.

A joy, a depression, a meanness,
some momentary awareness comes
as an unexpected visitor.

Welcome and entertain them all!
Even if they are a crowd of sorrows,
who violently sweep your house
empty of its furniture,
still, treat each guest honorably.
He may be clearing you out
for some new delight.

The dark thought, the shame, the malice.
meet them at the door laughing and invite them in.

Be grateful for whatever comes.
because each has been sent
as a guide from beyond.[5]

JELALUDDIN RUMI, TRANSLATION BY COLEMAN BARKS

CASE STUDY: GRACE'S JOURNEY

Our souls seek evolution, transformation, elevation, and transmutation until we humans get it right. Meaning, until we create a safe container for our soul in this body, we will be blocked in understanding the truth of who we are as a spiritual being. As an illustration, one of my clients, a middle-aged professional woman I'll call Grace, had discovered my work and was interested in integrating a psychotherapeutic session with shamanic healing. When she came in, Grace immediately became aware of her dissonance "traversing the two worlds." Her human life had been full of betrayal, struggle, abuse, and secrets, yet she said that she felt as though her soul needed these lessons for her growth. As we worked together on the High Holy Day of Yom Kippur, we experienced her emergence into the greater understanding of her soul's purpose in the world. In her human personality, Grace wanted to hide and talk about her frustrations and disappointments with her two children. Yet, as she did this, I brought awareness to her repetitive cycles of pain and suffering. She then started to listen inside to the voice of her soul, which was whispering, "You are a leader. Stop following others and clear out your path."

Immediately, she realized the need to ground the soles of her feet on the earth and experience her presence here on this physical plane. Eventually, Grace related that she was able to experience the crown of her head opening to the expansiveness of the sky, the ethereal realm, the Soul Realm. Soon after, she saw a forest with frogs, salamanders, and sun and light energies (in her inner vision). She allowed herself to be transfigured into a new being. Grace spoke of this as "my initiation into my own emergence of my future." The infinity symbol arrived to seal the energies from north to south, east to west in her internal structure. Rather than moving these balancing energies out into the world, she wanted to keep them for herself and chose to "zipper them up to contain them in my body, because I really need them for myself right now." This was the wisdom of her soul speaking and the clarity of the truth of what she really needed for this specific point in time. Grace needed to stay inside herself for the session and work with the beings from the Soul Realm that appeared, eager to support her flourishing into new emergence of being.[6] This session's focus was intrapsychic rather than interpersonal.

In Grace's session, "the battle with love," as she called it, allowed love to transcend her fears and enabled her to return to her own self-love from a place of open heart. She was able to call in communication and clarity from the Soul Realm about what was needed for her next steps. Recalling the words of Wilhelm Reich, "Knowledge of that which is alive can alone banish terror,"[7] she affirmed her mission: to allow the power of love to banish years of stored terror and fear in her body. She was able to release the historical imprint steeped in trauma and abuse so that she could emerge into her soul's full aliveness and creative expression. I was reminded of Rumi's words: "Your task is not to seek for love, but merely to seek and find all the barriers within yourself that you have built against it."[8] As my beloved yoga teacher often affirms, every interaction is either an expression of love—or a cry for love. Our souls remind us constantly that love really is the essence of all life. As we deepen in understanding this great mystery, things simplify and we learn to trust that we really don't have to figure out all the details. The process of life does unfold clearly and the pathway can be lit as we learn to honor the value of one incremental step at a time. Our task is to do our daily meditative practice to stay connected with the Soul Realm— this requires self-discipline and a supportive, like-minded community.

But What If the Problem Is That My Partner Is Not My Soul Mate?

Case Study: Connor's Search

Ultimately, your soul's desire is that its destiny will transcend any circumstances life brings your way. Understand that your soul's voice will be distinctively different from the reactive conversation expressing the conditioning of your human personality's narrative; it is initially quieter, gently sparring with the human woundedness, talking back to the lies we have accepted about our limitations. If we allow this dialogue, it will confirm our soul's insistence that Infinity's knowledge be integrated and housed within the body. One common example of this is the case of the couple in a long-term marriage, over fifteen years, with children, in which the husband, whom I'll call Connor, reports that he needs to leave the marriage because he has found his "soul mate." This could mean that Connor's soul, despite logic and reason, is seeking a path other than the life he and his family are now living. But these sorts of cases are quite complex.

Upon further investigation, I realize that Connor does not even know his own soul, much less hold an accurate perception of what "soul mate" would really mean (I think this is what the emphasis on finding a soul mate is all about. People are often searching for their own long-lost souls). The task at this point is to help the individual learn to access, contain, and embody his own soul first, and then further investigate the myriad possibilities of what is really going on. Often, it is the vacancy of connection to our own souls that leads, often compels, us to search in futility for soul mates outside ourselves. Many are looking to fill the gaping hole caused by the lack of attachment with their own soul. My suggestion is that we slow down and first learn to attend to the attachment with our own soul, as primary soul mate to ourselves. Then from this connection we find soul mate, soul family, soul tribe. Once we truly know our own soul, we can move consciously into the world and build a larger soul family in our extended environmental field, potentially creating a "more right" world globally as we attend to raising consciousness through our unique individual contribution.

When clients come to me for therapy, they are usually seeking some sort of immediate relief. Because we live in a culture that is accustomed to quick fixes, people often seek a flip-of-the-switch cure and have difficulty committing to the disciplined work of connecting to and dialoguing with their own soul. Many clients seek healing from the trauma, clarity in the confusion, peace in the chaos, or longing resolved. It is important to remember that conscious embodiment of cognition and emotion will foster a psychological safety in the body as container, which then will foster an opportunity to connect to our soul's unraveling. The best relief one can find is to finally come home to the soul in the body. As we heal individually, we will then better heal communally, understanding that, paradoxically, we are both alone and never alone, as we are both individual and communal creatures seeking separateness and togetherness within good community.

From this inner space of the soul's regenerative powers of renewal, we learn how to feed ourselves and the world. We begin to trust that the River of Life is always flowing for us and that this river can be trusted. It is our inability to foster attachment with our soul that creates the break with it. As we learn to allow the flow of our soul's ascension to feed our evolutionary movement, we begin to transform inertia into life, immobilization into action, sleep into awakening. Vitality awakens life within us, and as we engage with the outside, in the environmental field, our broader community is positively infused with soulful characteristics. Our souls are, by nature, evolutionary beings seeking to transform darkness into light, fragmentation into unification—within this body, the body of the self *and* the body of soulful community. This is the true enlightenment that shamanism addresses in its methodology of release-and-retrieval into the soul.

One word of caution (gleaned from listening for far too many years to our universal human struggle): a lack of awareness regarding true soul attachment can lead to wanderlust, bad decisions, and painful consequences that could be abated if one would learn to attach *first* to one's own soul. Once attached, we can seek the wisdom of our own soul to practically guide us through life's complex decisions. Over the years, I have witnessed many "soul-mates" who have had meaningful encounters with each other but are often unable to materialize their relationship on this physical plane in an enduring, committed way. The experience of "earth mates" with mutual development of soul seems to be the human journey that I observe as a practical reality for many couples. There are a few soul mates that end up coupling for the adult life cycle, but in my experience this is rare. I often see earth mates coupling initially around human "physical plane" issues; then, the presenting challenge for the couple (in practicing mature love) is to integrate the life of the soul into the relationship. Because of each person's woundedness colliding within the couple, this often presents many challenges. Understandably, these matters are complicated and require time and wisdom to process the multitude of factorial layers of truth. If you are in an "earth mate" relationship, my advice would be to try to continue to bring your soul's expression into the relationship, to integrate both earth and soul into the life of the partnership while at the same time supporting your partner in his or her soul's emergence.

DAILY LIFE AS MYSTICAL EXPERIENCE

"A long time ago, before anything had a name, we didn't know that we were man or woman, human or animal, male or female. When the wild reeds bowed their heads in the wind, we bowed our heads too, for it was the same spirit—breath that breathed through us every second, every hour, every day of our lives. At dawn when the brilliant orange squash blossom opened gently, gently at the first warm kiss of the sun, we too opened our eyes and uncurled from sleep, stretching wise, stretching far, rejoicing as every part of our bodies came to life again."[9]

PENINA V. ADELMAN

Viewed from this perspective, everyday life is the "playground of inquiry" for the soul's embodied expression. As we welcome the circumstances of our lives with compassionate embrace, we learn to accept and befriend these circumstances as opportunities for our soul's evolution. We see through a different lens, and our lives make more sense, with the help of an internal wisdom. When we allow ourselves the ongoing experiment of direct mystical experience with the Absolute, we learn to listen with new ears to each conversation and observe with new eyes our reactivity from the human imprint of our past wounding. We have the potential to experience nature's elements as medicine—balm for the soul—in renewing, supportive ways. This medicine, as it comes in, provides the basis for the talking back to the human reactivity, diminishing fear, distrust, panic, and anxiety. One example of using daily life as meditative practice would look something like this: If it's a misty day, try breathing into the water element, focusing on its cleansing properties for your body. Internally imagine a washing away of an angry embittered attitude or an inability to forgive someone who has harmed or disappointed you.

When we experience our days with an open receptivity toward nature and the life of our soul, nature's elements and the surprise conversations we encounter spontaneously with people who cross our path unexpectedly can awaken our souls to a transformative experience. We become sensitized to soul activity everywhere, especially in nature and in the surprise elements within spontaneity and openness. Transcendence and new beliefs will be kindled, offering us an invitation to perceive the world with new eyes. We learn that soul activity can be trusted after all, even in the physicality of daily living. Ethereal "ahh-haahs" can be grounded and rooted in this physical plane as information travels from the upper and lower worlds, informing our middle-world existence. Our souls teach us how to answer back to the skeptic self as we commune with the Soul Realm through daily embodied experiment, learning that the information offered is valuable and can be acted upon.

Drawing from cognitive-behavioral therapy and dialectical behavior therapy techniques (CBT/DBT), supporting a "talking-back self" nurtures the understanding that the wounded, limited being (of the human personality) can dialogue with the voice of soul. In this conversation we find that we are permanently changed. As we learn to give our soul the final voice, allowing it to be "top dog," our cognition, emotion, and behaviors move into alignment with the destiny of our soul's wisdom in the choices we make. As a result, we find ourselves moving in the world like an arrow; our thoughts, beliefs, emotions, and actions are aligned with our power to manifest, and we experience congruency from within.

It is important that we honor all aspects of ourselves as we work to encounter our souls. As we welcome our skeptic self, we benefit from acknowledging and embracing our wounded self, the part of us that is embedded in habitual patterns of distraction, interruption, avoidance, rationalization, and confusion. The wounded self has lived so long beneath its comforting veil—as a means of self-protection—that the thought of lifting the veil can seem frightening. There is value in bringing all aspects of our full self, just as they are, into the light of compassionate embrace in order to support a dialogue between them, in the interiority within. In Gestalt theory, we refer to this as the multiplicity of the self. This is not like when we were young and perhaps forced to attend church services in our "Sunday best." In the Soul Realm, we are cherished as we are, seeking transmutation and transcendence, knowing that we are greeted in the truth of our human reality. It is understood that this human realm of reality is constantly seeking to be transformed and transcended.

The seed of memory within us (our soul) discerns between what is truth and what is not truth. The place of remembering and then forgetting truth is the human experience devoid of the soul (a symptom of soul loss). Wanting to know while still afraid to know, desiring to see yet hoping to stay veiled is not the realm of soul. This is the human dance of fear, avoidance, and inner conflict acting out a childhood game of hide-and-seek. This experience is often referred to as a "double-bind" (in psychology). These are mixed messages full of ambivalence and tension that simultaneously draw us close yet push us away, creating a veiled, trapped existence devoid of contact or connection with our soul. Many of us have been raised in homes and have relationships full of these double binds and mixed messages, which keep us trapped. We learn to accept cognitive dissonance as normal when, in reality, these are the exact moments when humanity can potentially meet Divinity and commune in an informative way, which can help remove inner conflicts. Unfortunately, these fleeting moments are lost for many of us because we are often so comfortable in avoiding contact with our own soul that we miss a moment to commune internally. As part of our spiritual practice, we can either allow ourselves to be drawn closer to the true voice of soul or we can allow our fear and skepticism to push us away. If we practice receptivity with the Soul Realm, the magic of transformation will offer its medicine, anticipating that our human experience will be transformed by Divine Truth. Often that which we are most afraid of and spend years of our lives pushing away, trying to avoid, is the content of the Soul Realm trying to reveal itself to us directly. Remember, this is the path of direct revelation often utilizing nature (and the elements) to speak to our true nature.

INNER PERCEPTION OF TREE AS SELF-IMAGE: THE HUMAN BODY AS THE BRIDGE—ROOTED IN THE EARTH AND EXPANSIVE IN THE SKY

The model of the Tree of Life reminds us that as humans we are both *human* and *Spirit*. As tree people, we are grounded in the earth element while simultaneously open to the ever-expansive ether/air element. From this perspective, it is often helpful to image the human body as a bridge, with our feet on the earth and our head in the heavens. Our inner energy body, *as a central pillar of energy, with its seven major centers*, is located along the spinal column in the etheric body, connecting us to earth and sky. We learn through meditative practice that we are always experiencing the pulse or vibration of these energy centers, which are believed to hold memory, both bitter and sweet. It is through this pillar that our energy flows and manifests outward into the external world—or it remains blocked and does not manifest our dreams and intentions but rather our deeply held fears and worries. As you work with your breath, imagine it moving, like the infinity symbol, from north to south, east to west, and then begin to feel the movement circling like the sun or the moon or the frame of the drum (within your solar plexus, your center). You will begin to experience your own rhythm rocking you gently into a more relaxed state as you learn to embody the release-and-retrieval process of the breath, releasing or letting go of that which must leave the container of your body and saying hello to or welcoming that which you want to retrieve (inner peace, calm, integration, or healing). Imagine in your inner vision the infinity symbol moving you toward soul attachment—moving from detachment to attachment in a back-and-forth movement, with imagery from your soul's intelligence. Inner awareness of this movement supports your moment-to-moment presence with your internal experience just as it wants to unfold, without your having to censor or block its clarity. Remember that there is always aid from the Soul Realm in reattaching with our soul in the everyday experience of daily life. We need only ask.

The Eight Kundalini Chakras

❖ **1ˢᵗ Chakra:** BASE/ROOT. Earth element/Smell. Red. The first chakra corresponds to the area of the rectum. It relates to the instinctive drive to fulfill one's most primitive needs for belonging, connectivity, and survival, linking us to the reproductive areas.

❖ **2ⁿᵈ Chakra:** SACRAL. Water element / Taste. Orange. The second chakra controls the pelvic area, sex organs, potency of manifestation in the world, and bodily fluid functions. Also associated with the adrenal glands, it controls all solid parts of the body—spinal column, bones, teeth, and nails—as well as the blood and the restoration of the cells, kidneys, and bladder.

❖ **3ʳᵈ Chakra:** SOLAR PLEXUS. Fire element / Sight. Yellow. The third chakra corresponds to the area around the navel and the solar plexus. It is the principal storehouse of energy, which explains why it is considered the seat of power, willfulness, health, and vitality. Personal growth can be interrupted at this center by fear, greed, and one's need for personal power. Also associated with the pancreas, it controls the liver, digestive system, stomach, spleen, gall bladder, muscles, autonomic nervous system, and lower back.

The first three chakras are known as "the lower triangle." They represent the level at which the majority of people function or react in the world, from the wounded imprint (which is not the place of soul attachment). This is the realm of senses and feelings; what one feels is considered the highest level of truth. Decisions are based on the reality of the moment, and a person's base needs, not his or her higher ideals or values, are the guide. With my model, we are consistently trying to raise our energy and awareness to the fourth center of consciousness, the heart, which informs all other chakras as the seat of the soul.

❖ 4ᵗʰ Chakra: HEART. Green. Air Element / Touch. The fourth chakra lies in the area of the sternum and relates to one's capacity to experience and express love and compassion. It is associated with the thymus and controls the heart, circulation, immune system, lower lungs, rib cage, skin, upper back, and hands.

❖ 5ᵗʰ Chakra: THROAT. Blue. Air element / Sound. The fifth chakra relates to one's ability to communicate directly. It is associated with the thyroid and controls the jaw, neck, throat, voice, airways, upper lungs, nape of the neck, and arms.

❖ 6ᵗʰ Chakra: THIRD EYE. Indigo. Ether element / Light. The sixth chakra is related to knowledge, wisdom, and the development of one's intuition. It is associated with the pituitary gland and controls the endocrine system, left brain hemisphere, left eye, nose, ears, sinuses, and parts of the nervous system.

❖ 7ᵗʰ Chakra: CROWN. Violet, gold, and/or white. Ether element/ Thought. The seventh chakra is located at the top of the head, around where the "soft spot" is on a newborn. It corresponds to the pineal gland, the master gland of the body, and is related to self-realization and the experience of union with the entire universe. This is the realm of boundlessness, where one can live beyond time, space, and causation. This chakra controls the cerebrum, right brain hemisphere, central nervous system, and right eye.

In kundalini yoga, there is an eighth chakra, also known as the auric field; it is the magnetic energy surrounding the human being. According to Gurmukh, in her book *The 8 Human Talents*, this is what provides the "hue" or "glow" of a human and can reflect the general mental and physical health of a person. Traditionally, in other systems, the aura has not always been looked at as a chakra. In kundalini yoga, it is recognized as a center of consciousness that, once activated, allows a person to easily experience realms beyond the physical body. The aura is also considered to be the externalization of the interiority of the chakra's health and functions as a magnetic field, magnifying in the environmental field from the inner core.

WHAT IF I CAN'T SEE ANYTHING?

When we read the writings of the great mystics or people who claim to have seen the "face of the Divine," typically they describe a great white light or they speak of the Beloved quite intimately, as if the intimacy is always there. Often, in truth, when beginning this practice, we initially confront the void, the impasse, and see nothing but darkness. Gestalt theory calls this moment of potential conception the "*fertile void*," reminding us that *something* is just around the corner if we are patient. As my dear co-facilitator of a group said over twenty-five years ago, "*There is something about nothing.*" Until we learn to stay with the emptiness long enough, or sit with the nothingness patiently in stillness, or drum with the vacancy into connection, we will come away empty and frustrated. In other words, we don't always see the great white light or any other images right away. This is a spiritual practice and one that requires discipline, so be gentle with yourself in this process. Eventually, we move from emptiness into spaciousness. As we remain committed to this practice, we find ourselves walking a mystical path and experiencing a steady and unwavering communion with our souls. Even in the face of the "dry periods" or "the dark nights," we remember what we know and are reminded not to give up. We learn to trust that we can pursue our own soul, like we would our lover, until we receive that which we seek. Sometimes the search takes us all the way back to the hidden memories of our younger selves. Our early childhood years often hold the imaginative/magical selves who know instinctively that this magical realm can be trusted. In my clinical experience, it is common that once these younger selves are retrieved and integrated into the adult self, this work becomes more easily graspable. The lost selves, who are all too comfortable hiding, often need to be called out with tenderness, invited to live safely in the body. Since these lost selves believe it is best to be in hiding and to not be seen, it is quite a process for them to learn to trust and to welcome that it is, in fact, okay, even delightful to be seen. Being seen in turn promotes seeing into the Soul Realm. Once these lost aspects of self are retrieved through committed, patient discovery, sight into the invisible realms becomes easier. This unification into the adult self of the chronologically young selves must occur internally in order for you to launch more deeply into the Soul Realm.

Once we learn to comfortably spend time alone in meditation and reflection, we settle into embracing the internal quiet of stillness. We quickly learn to respect and trust that we are never alone. The "aloneness" becomes the "all-oneness" as we embrace our multifaceted interiority. The birds chirping outdoors also remind us that the Soul Realm awaits our communion. The stillness speaks to us, calling, "Come linger a while." The leaves gently blowing in the wind are our inspiration, reminding us to stay rooted in the earth and yet dance with the element of air, the sky. The world of nature becomes more alive to us as we learn to listen to it and begin to understand that nature is always waiting to reveal itself to our true nature. It is our inability to see and trust the flow of the process into the unknown that furthers our detachment from ourselves, the natural world, and our very souls. We will, in fact, move *through* the unknown once we allow ourselves to move *into* the unknown.

But in order to do this, we need our internal supports and our tool kit (the tools discussed in this book). With practice, we learn to trust that there is always something on the other side of the unknown if we allow our soul to be an active presence informing our life's decisions. The process of letting go and allowing ourselves to regularly experience the movement from unknowing to knowing is the primary tool that reinforces trust in how it all works. Allowing the movement of Infinity (working internally with the healing infinity symbol as a tool) to carry us from knowing (seeing) to unknowing (unseeing) and back to knowing, if we let it, builds our courage. Just as bicep curls exercise the upper body, we are exercising our soul, learning to better understand the mystery of how it works. Losing ourselves in the process of letting go of the busy brain (or the monkey mind, as the yogis call it) helps us become open to perceiving the world in new ways. In other words, as my wise co-facilitator said to me when we were running a multi-family therapy group together, "You have to allow yourself to be lost before you can be found."[7]

As you learn to listen to your soul and experience the opening of your heart to receptivity, you will begin to experience your own soul more clearly, often through visual images and inner auditory messages. The small voice that sends a brief one-liner in one ear and out the other will appear more often. As one client described in session, "It is as if the wind is moving from one ear to another, on the inside, clearing things out." She reported that she felt as if her brain were expanding. If you allow yourself to trust this inner intelligence, you will begin to answer back to the voice of self-doubt and skepticism, because you will see the shifts occurring in your interiority, remembering that this work clears from the inside out. Often you will observe yourself taking different actions in your life, managing yourself differently in your relationships.

LISTENING WITHIN

Our soul wants to know that we are listening and that we will receive its information faithfully. Otherwise, the information will be withheld from us. If we do not present with open eyes to see and listening ears to hear, it seems as though the Soul Realm declares us unsafe containers not yet ready to receive these gems, for they must be used wisely. There are "rules of engagement" (in this practice), similar to those in a human relationship in which one partner stops sharing with the other partner because she or he is perceived as not listening and not receiving without judgment. The flavor of our relationship with the Soul Realm mirrors human relationships in quality and character. Just as in marriage, friendship, family and work relations, the daily practices of openness, listening to understand, feeding connection, and trusting all fuel deepening exchange and information flow, so it is with the Soul Realm. With time and experience, we learn that this information can be trusted and integrated, and then we can begin to act on it. As we acknowledge the soul's wisdom to be truth, additional knowledge begins to unfold; the inner knowing becomes more specific and clear.

OPENING TO POTENTIALITY:
THE BLUE SKY MEDICINE—THE AIR ELEMENT

Within a shamanic framework, use of the frame drum mimics the beating of the heart and we move, magically, into "the pulse of Infinity," a rhythm, *a flow of soul-time*, otherwise known as a "shamanic state of consciousness." This is the state in which we develop eyes to see into the unseen universe. The research shows that as we deepen into this theta brain wave activity, we open and expand our consciousness from that which we typically experience as reality. As we deepen into this spiritual seer lens, we begin to recognize our soul's voice, which enables us to decode our soul's information. We allow data from otherworldly places to flow freely and be received rather than blocked. We do not need a frame drum to actualize these soul states, but it certainly can help facilitate speedier access. As we deepen this skill set, we can learn to drop into a more relaxed state and consciously access the Soul Realm, wherever we are. Even in the middle of a roundtable discussion or a boardroom meeting, we can deepen into our breath and access this realm to obtain wise information for practical business matters. Or, while having an argument with a loved one, we might go inside and practice these tools in order to become better at being a listening presence, offering greater empathy and compassion.

Each living being has a soul with a distinct purpose, a driving message that will not go away. Typically, the soul lives by the laws of a different land—so much so that the monkey mind (based on rational, logical standards) will often think the soul's information is dubious. In other words, *the busy brain is a highly trained skeptic of the soul.* The soul, however, has an intelligence all its own and is quite persistent in speaking up, even if in a gentle voice, though it will also silence itself if not listened to over time. When denial of the soul occurs, disease and addictions will magnify and physical illness can sometimes worsen. If the soul does not obtain revelation of its true identity, and if information is not accepted and embodied by the human personality, then dis-ease, in its many forms, will be inevitable and the need to numb oneself with multiple addictions will ensue. Essentially, addictions are about the cessation of connection with the soul, the pursuit of "fillers" because the emptiness is too painful. The challenge is to learn how to delve inside to fill the soul's empty spaces with luminous knowing. The awakening of the soul happens in its own time with its own process, which is to be respected—but we do have to *do something* to aid in this unfolding. We have to "show up" and allow this something to unravel.

SOUL ATTACHMENT

If you live your life from soul attachment and conscious knowledge of your soul's destiny, yours will be a very different life than one lived from detachment of soul. Practicing self-awareness is a key to seeing yourself as you move on the continuum of attachment/detachment (a back-and-forth process), which is the spectrum of soul activity (as we are both human and divine in these bodies). As you practice these tools daily, you will achieve greater purpose, meaning, and satisfaction as your soul attends to its destiny, on its own terms. Even in the face of increased "difficulties" on the earthly plane, the soul will offer a calm assurance that all is well. This is because the soul carries a perspective that transcends the human experience. This provides an awareness (infused by the soul's perception) and an acceptance of the situation, even when the human experience is full of fear, worry, and/or anxiety. The soul, as divine personality, will feed the self with expanded, wise, and empowering information rather than the lies, limitations, and constriction of the wounded personality with its destructive habitual patterns of thought and action.

The one condition of the soul is that we have to be willing to do "the work." This daily discipline promises to lead to an experience that is real, generating confidence and belief. This will foster self-mastery, trust, and confidence in the gnosis, so that these are not hidden mysteries or fleeting insights but rather a steady stream of vital information. Remember that your soul is eager to give you help, referred to as "medicine" in the shamanic world. The ancestors, spirit guides, animal spirits, and ancient teachers love you and want to commune with you. In the same way that a parent wants to help its child, these beings are eager to aid us in this challenging human journey of our embodied soul in human flesh, in this daily physical world. It's as if the Cosmic Soul is communicating with individual souls, encouraging growth so that a higher purpose might be achieved. The ancient battle of darkness versus light is addressed as Soul suggests, "Promote goodness. Pursue peace. Give love. Be light." This is the path of embodied enlightenment, where we learn to talk back to the messages of darkness, woundedness, shadow, and disowned unconsciousness, which seeks to inhabit and rule within our body's interiority.

While the Christian church doesn't directly teach a doctrine of conscious development of the soul, many mystical references exist in sacred texts. Jesus did say, "Ye must be born again" (John 3:7), which conjures up reflection of the birth experience revisited daily, from life to death to rebirth. As Plato reminds us, movement from the River of Forgetfulness into soul attachment is a daily midwifery. The power of sharing this in community is, of course, ideal and is what "good religion" or constructive community can provide. The comfort of a community of spiritual seekers "in it together" helps the body of believers function as a unified whole and can challenge and invite each of us, in our soul's full expression, to see and be seen. It is within the community, ideally, that we embody our soul's destiny and learn to respect that the finger needs the hand and the tiny pinky toe is essential in supporting the foot. We discover in good community that what we are working on within our individual body—wholeness, integration, soul expression, and love—can and will be tested as we learn to practice in relatedness what we believe. Unfortunately, because so many systems function destructively and do not truly support the liberty of authentic soul expression, there are times when some may have to leave their beloved community because they have outgrown that community's dogma. These people will, most likely, seek to find their soul's sustenance by building community elsewhere. This is a very painful yet necessary process in the soul's ascension. Other souls may be found, in the more progressive denominations, working on issues of social justice, world poverty, world peace, and world hunger. Integrated souls are typically more interested in the global world than in their own individual advancement; therefore, the moral prescriptions and narrow limitations of institutionalized religious systems no longer work to feed soul life in nurturing ways.

As we age, our soul is more open to complexity and is at home with deeper mystery, which often lives beyond narrowly defined religious confines and institutionalized, dominating dogma. This is why integrating multiple spiritual traditions or the arts becomes more captivating as a soul matures. This is a journey of the soul's ascent into expansion beyond the walls of confining dogma. The challenge is that most of us have been shaped by socio-cultural systems rooted in our dependence on "authoritative insider information." This conditioning trains us to be fearful of trusting our own soul's revelation. The difficulties in accessing the sacred knowledge are further increased as many of the enlightened masters pass on information only orally, from teacher to student, and a select few are the lucky ones. Knowing that not everyone will respect the teachings and that some may seek to use the powers unwisely, some schools of sacred knowledge and spiritual traditions have been understandably guarded about who receives this sacred information. We must act in responsible ways when we practice the shamanic path, understanding that this is the path of direct revelation and requires our utmost respect for its wisdom.

When we are given the honor of dialoguing with the Divine, we cannot take the experience lightly. I have found that the Soul Realm will go into hiding, as if checking to see if one is truly committed to the sacred path. When we are given information from the great Ascended Masters like Jesus, Mother Mary, the buddhas and bodhisattvas, Crone Woman, Confucius, Buddhist monks, or the sages and magicians, it is important to practice gratitude for what comes, while at the same time asking that more be given. We must learn not to be afraid to ask for more. When more is withheld and the Soul Realm speaks in confusing metaphors, there is often learning there as well. It appears that the direct revelation happens one step at a time, as if a larger puzzle were coming together one piece at a time. Spiritual growth is about learning not only to practice patience but to value patience as a necessary place to land—as time in the Soul Realm is different from time in the physical plane. Holding on to trust and belief in our soul's existence as the unknown unfolds, one step at a time, is the wisdom path of Sacred Mystery.

When we move into dialogue with our soul, all beings in the Soul Realm unify in light and love and seek to shed their healing light on our dark crevices. Shadow is transformed, disowned parts of self are owned and embodied, while wounded aspects of self and soul are healed. As fragmented parts of soul are brought home, it is believed (and it has been my observation with my clients) that they are then reconfigured, on a cellular level, to create an experience of internal wholeness and cohesiveness. Whether the wise saints and sages of old, the mystics and prophets of all ages, the angels or the animals or the elementals, all the divine beings appear to help us come into alignment with our own soul, offering aid and guidance for our personal quest for knowledge, wisdom, and enlightenment.

THE INHALE AND EXHALE BREATH AS LINKED TO INFINITY

The very simple act of breathing is an exercise in this daily practice as we remember that it is always available and accessible to us moment by moment in our bodies. Attending to our breath helps us awaken our awareness of how often we are living our lives from a place of "fight, flight or freeze"—known as the "survival response." Many, if not most, of us have learned the value of fighting for ourselves as a means of survival. We sing out loud proudly with the pop song's words, "No one can take away your right / To fight and never surrender," often proud of how far we have come, fighting our way to the top. What we don't realize is that in this fighter mentality, we are usually not in an internal state of relaxation, ease, or connection with our soul. Our breath is impaired, with destructive consequences for our brain's processing, our body awareness, and our spirit's soaring. Science is now more certain than ever that when we don't breathe deeply into our abdomen, the organs of our internal body are negatively affected. Many of us are accustomed to living our days with some sort of anticipatory anxiety, waiting for something bad to happen, for "the other shoe to drop."

It continues to amaze me that even in times of ease and life-is-good states of coupledom, partners still fear and worry, and distrust seems to bubble up. As humans, we seem to be more "uncomfortably comfortable" waiting for the painful issues to surface. As we learn to change this model, we learn that life is a continual flow of unlearning old patterns of reactivity while relearning new imprints of vitality of soul expression, opening ourselves to living daily from this newfound integration and inner peace.

DAILY EXERCISE: CONSCIOUS, DELIBERATE BREATH WORK

A helpful practice to work with is to bring concentrated attention to the "inhale breath" and the "exhale breath." We remind ourselves to deliberately and consciously open to the Soul Realm through each inhale breath. Many refer to the breath as the primordial, sacred rhythm of Spirit. Within Christianity, it is the Holy Spirit, like a white dove, which symbolizes the breath of life. Many of us have learned to become mindless about our breath, unaware of living in a state of "life and death" survival, exhibiting tightness of breath. As you think about the inhale breath—the taking in of the life force—as *receiving life and spaciousness,* you will want to consciously breathe from your belly; and as you exhale, practice letting go, *releasing* old habits or habitual destructive behaviors that interrupt the attachment with your soul. As you breathe out, you release what needs to go in order to make space inside for new "information," creating a renewed spaciousness for an open heart. I suggest doing this while resting your right hand on your belly and your left hand on your heart. It is useful to have the thumb of your right hand touching the pinky of your left hand while stretching the pinky on your right hand as far down as you can toward your belly button and stretching the thumb on your left hand as high up toward your clavicle as you are able. The extended stretch helps bring heightened awareness to this core aspect of your being that you are seeking to fill up, like a balloon, with breath. You will begin to notice that your inhale breath breathes in new thoughts, fresh emotional states, and a certain calm that will eventually inform your actions by this enlightened gnosis. *As we breathe more deeply into our abdominal breath—some call it the breath of fire—we understand this once latent act to be organizing our interiority into a willful force, inspiring our soul's flame to ignite. It is common to feel a lightness of being as we release from our hold that which is no longer needed.*

CHAPTER 4
HEALING FROM THE INSIDE OUT

> *There is no death. Only a change of worlds.*
>
> CHIEF SEATTLE

THESE FINITE BONDS TEACH US TO EMBRACE THE INFINITE

The ancient yogis believed we must die every day in order to better comprehend how to fully live. I've been practicing yoga since 1997 and it is only now that I am beginning to feel as though I understand what this means. Since turning fifty-five, I have become much more mindful of my mortality. Life has become more precious, and the pursuit of those things that feed the life force is acutely in my awareness as I encourage myself, my clients, and my loved ones to pay close attention to those activities that actually feed good feeling and aliveness. With the practice of each yoga class, I am learning to deepen even more fully into a breath that I am certain I will not find. In these moments, I feel that I must leave the class early from sheer exhaustion; then suddenly I feel a burst of new space in my body. Often, this space feels like a quarter of an inch, perhaps even only an eighth, but nonetheless, I feel something inside like a release of an old memory, a stretch into new horizons. An insight clarifies. An image appears and I am certain the Soul Realm is with me, talking to me. The ancient yogis certainly understood the value of coming into the finite body to expand and reach the Infinite. We all can remember this, whether we practice yoga or not, as we practice accessing Mystery in our own way each and every day.

PINNACLE OF UNION

Lovemaking and sexual union are physical, transparent reminders of the finite merging with the Infinite in the flesh. Through orgasmic experience, the human container opens and often remembers much more union than we are usually conscious of in our daily lives. Again, the wisdom of incarnation is the physical reminder that we find union

71

with divine expansiveness *in these bodies* rather than in the heavens. *This is the soul's core message.* Our bodies teach us that transcendence seeks to be inhabited in nature. Ideally, the true nature of our being is found through authenticity, vulnerability, and transparency. When one body meets another in sexual union and we experience oneness, often we cry out in orgasm, "Oh, my God." This is because the moment actually touches the Infinite, the world of Soul, and whether we call it God or Soul or Spirit or good sex—we know, experientially, that we are in the presence of something far greater than ourselves. *The lesson of incarnation is to inhabit the body while housing the Infinite, unraveling the message of the soul's unity with the Divine.* We must learn how to reach toward the expansive sky while grounding in the physical realm of earth energies, the flesh. Daily life becomes the lesson in decoding otherworldly information as wisdom flows through our crown into our bones, reminding us of our connection with the Divine. While we are still embodied in our finite flesh, searching, even struggling, to stay on track with our soul's purpose in the world, our destiny is unveiled one vision at a time.

As many of us have been fortunate to experience through a positive, expansive sexual union, there is a life-force energy that has the potential to awaken and empower an internal flame. This powerful energy can incite wisdom and compassion, consciousness, and concern for the larger community. "Kundalini energy" and "chi" are terms for this life force that sits coiled at the bottom of our spine, waiting to be awakened and enlivened to its powerful healing medicine. It uncoils only when the masculine and feminine forces are balanced and intertwined; otherwise it sits with tension in the base, like a closed, tight fist. Often, my clients will describe this potent awakening energy traveling from the base of the spine and spreading all throughout their internal energetic body, even into their fingertips and their toes. When kundalini medicine is doing its work, the snake or the winged serpent will appear in the inner vision, applying its medicine and helping us shed the old and awaken the new. The unwrapping or unraveling experience will be viscerally felt as the kundalini travels up from the base to the crown, north to south then east to west, then eventually traveling in a circular motion in the general area of the solar plexus. You may experience this alone or within a coupling experience. Often, as in tantric sex, this "pinnacle of union" (which looks something like the diagram on page 74) will appear in the inner vision, with flames of fire on the east and west sides and one big flame burning bright at the top. This symbol often appears when the sacred masculine and sacred feminine are most intertwined and in balance and the inner flames of fire, passion, and clarity—the inner sun—are being reignited.

During soul-retrieval work, it is common for people to have sexual, sensual bursts of awakening from the sacrum, traveling up the spine, sometimes in more concentrated ways at different phases of the life cycle. In shamanic healing, similar to yoga and ecstatic sexual experience, the kundalini—which is the Sanskrit word for "corporeal energy"—is awakened on a regular basis as the energy centers release, freeing immobilized memories of woundedness, shame, fear, or abuse along with habitual patterns of pain and suffering. You may even feel slight tremors or a shaking as old, unneeded energies are released. A feeling of electrifying current running along the spine may be experienced. One client, whom I will call Kate, experienced this at first as the entire back side of her body going numb. Then as the healing energies came through, she began to feel like stretching and she saw vibrant purples and blues. Kate reported that she began to feel her back body to be more connected to her front body. She could feel the way in which her spine was providing her with "backbone." She also noticed a retrieval of a renewed vitality from the base and felt her hips more and her feet better planted and rooted in the earth. She then felt the expansive energies moving into her brain and later said, "It felt like my brain was doing a bicep curl. It was as if I needed to have my mind exercised by something larger than me in order to reach a fuller potentiality."

These sensations fit into the category of kundalini rising, which is described as an unconscious, instinctive, or libidinal life force intimately connected to the vibration of the soul. In certain yoga Upanishads, the "lying, coiled serpent" awakens to cultivate the creative soul's highest potential to uphold values consistent with the spiritual world. It is reported by many that awakened kundalini results in deep meditation, enlightenment, ecstasy, or bliss. Upon awakening, you may even find yourself speaking truth with greater ease and clarity, congruence, and tenderness. This all arises from an inner alignment, in your body's interiority, with your soul's consciousness. Once it becomes embodied, like an

CASE STUDY: CLAIRE'S JOURNEY

I was recently working with an exhausted client, whom I'll call Claire, who was transitioning through a separation (a common case for me as a marriage and family therapist). As I was drumming for her, invoking her spirit guides and soul helpers to bring her aid and internal supports, Claire was very quickly surrounded (in her own inner vision of experience) by a "circle of power," images of Athena, mermaids, the water element, faeries, a jaguar/cougar/cat with big green eyes, the goddess Sekhmet, and a mighty angel. She immediately reported calm and wisdom, which came through her entire body, moving from her solar plexus out into every inch of space in her internal body. It is normal perhaps to be curious about these images. Who are they? Is she making them up with the power of her imagination? Or is there something indeed "real" about this experience—informed from a different reality? Only you will know the answers to these questions, if you allow yourself your own individual experience.

Claire later reported many visitations, especially by the great goddess who calls herself Sekhmet. She was the great protectress of Egypt, its kingship, and the divine order (Ma'at), a very powerful presence indeed. It is believed in Egyptian culture that Sekhmet oversees the preservation of the universe from chaos, the latter possibly represented by the snake she holds.[1] Sekhmet's name is the feminine form of a word meaning "the Powerful One" or "the Power," which is an idea expressed by her leonine head. Claire's report over the following months was that many of these forces were with her when she slept, when she daydreamed, and when she meditated, filling her with a sense of personal power, hope, and a courageous will to act in her own interest (and in support of her children's needs).

Claire's experience is consistent with the experiences of many of my mid-life clients who are in an uninvited situation, such as being the noninitiating partner of divorce, who find themselves in unwelcomed circumstances they never dreamed would become their experience. I have worked with these clients—who have been quickly sinking into the pit of despair and hopelessness, understandably feeling betrayed by both life and their spouses—together in shamanic states to retrieve power animals and spirit helpers so their souls can offer wisdom, guidance, and strength. Even while experiencing an extreme loss of material goods acquired throughout a lifetime and the loss of the stability that comes from life not being what it has always been, they surprisingly become alive, right before my eyes. A resurgence of vitality, awakened strength, and power, with a lightness of being emerges as their souls endure the emptying process and a spaciousness fills their spines with renewed backbone. This is a rebirth into expanded consciousness, or soul's ascension, even when initially an unwelcomed awakening. It is entirely possible that the soul has "called in" these circumstances as a plan of fulfillment of the person's life's destiny. Life and death—as in the life/ death/rebirth cycle—are mysteriously intertwined, one and the same, in the Soul Realm. Our souls are willing to die many deaths to ascend to our highest potential.

THE TWO WORLDS COLLIDE

As you dialogue more and more with the Soul Realm as a daily practice, you will begin to trust that the *unseen* world really can be *seen*; that the *formless* takes *form*; the *invisible* becomes *visible*. As you begin to comfortably traverse the two worlds, of the seen and the unseen, you begin to experience yourself, like the winged creature, moving with ease between earth and sky. You take flight and find your wings and begin to understand that there is far more to this than we know. Some have called this magick. Others, faith. Still more, spirituality or mysticism. My experience is that in the Soul Realm, these different traditions merge and work together for good, bringing healing and transcendence for those who seek. We see dimly at first, as we might find it difficult to thread the eye of a sewing needle. Then, the spiritual world opens, as if the Red Sea were parting or a portal allowed access, and the thick mist is lifted. Suddenly the unseen becomes more visible and interpretable to us and is no longer the land of the unseen, but is seen through the eyes of enlightened inner vision. In this magical place, we may see our career's next step unfolding. Or we may find clarity that it is indeed time to find forgiveness within for our spouse and deepen in the exercise of offering mature love toward our mate. Divination work can be done at moments like this, as the veil lifts and we see into a mirror dimly.

If we address this same issue from a psychological model, namely Gestalt theory, we learn that staying present in the impasse and sitting in stillness with the blankness or darkness of the void allows us to trust that there is something on the other side—a "something" in the "noth-ing," a fertility in the emptiness. Another Gestalt term, "death layer," or the darkness that we inevitably face when we sit in stillness, reminds us in its wisdom, that death is merely a necessary layer—a next step toward renewed birth—not necessarily the whole of an experience.

PERSISTENT DIALOGUE WITH THE SOUL REALM ASSURES THE VEIL WILL BE LIFTED

Each time we enter into dialogue with the Soul Realm, we are awakened to an unveiling process. The promise of our souls is that the veil will be lifted and we will see more clearly. As you recognize that you are the one that must ask to have the veil lifted in collaboration with your soul's helpers, envision the veil actually being lifted. Eventually, you will begin to see the same imaginal beings showing up repeatedly to help you. When I say that certain things must be done, I mean to offer the information not as dogma to be followed prescriptively but as guiding principles for rules of conduct. Over the years, I have learned to respect these principles in order to bring about the best result, just as with a love relationship in which you offer your partner respect, openness, and understanding and, most important, attend to them with your "listening ears." From this place of giving you also receive and benefit from the fruitful rewards of intimacy. The same is true in dialoguing with the Soul Realm. You will discover the possibility of mastering your own soul, which, just like your beloved lover, is never fully known but known through one enriching encounter at a time. These moments of rich and rewarding encounter are the foundation for closeness and attachment that can be trusted. The mystery of knowing and yet not fully knowing is always held in a fruitful tension, inviting us to go deeper and explore yet again the vastness of our souls. Each previous experience becomes the building block of trust in your soul's seed of memory.

VISUALIZATION: THE RIVER OF LIFE

Jesus answered and said to her, "Everyone who drinks of this water shall thirst again; but whoever drinks of the water that I shall give him shall never thirst; but the water that I shall give him shall become in him a well of water springing up to eternal life."

JOHN 4: 13, 14

Many traditional, indigenous societies believe that the ancient, mystical River of Life feeds inspiration, challenge, spontaneous surprise, and love, the great gifts necessary for a life well lived. An internal image of this river functions as supportive imagery, connecting us to our interiority of vitality, sustaining an active life within our inner world, which helps us talk back to soul loss, depression, stagnation, and resignation. As we meet the medicine of the water element, the flowing inner current of the River of Life reminds us to develop the capacity to be fluid and flexible like water, so that we do not suffer soul loss. This water imagery (sometimes as river, as ocean, as lake, or as waterfall) envelops the notion that, as we stay connected to our own truth flowing from within, we will grow from the inside out. The clarity of trusting that the River of Life always carries us can become a beacon, an internal lighthouse, that guides us and keeps our inner column, our core, aligned and lit. We experience this inner light, both up and down the spine, in the front body as well as the back body (often circling from top to bottom, inside and outside). We can even experience this inner light doing its magical medicine, like a sewing needle mending a hole. This internal medicine can integrate the five body splits and the blocked energy centers, or chakras, suffered through a lifetime of trauma. hurt, abuse, betrayal, and loss.

When we respond from this inner sphere of light and wisdom, we will see our human reactivity with an increased awareness and more consciously understand the wounded places within that are especially vulnerable, raw, and reactionary. We call these the "core wounds," in psychological terminology. These core wounds are the greatest enemy to the soul's voice, as they know exactly how to delude us with their comforting illusions, which keep us living in interrupted states of forgetfulness and unsatisfying, destructive, habitual patterns. As we develop an inner world that feeds us with light, love, and compassion, which is clearly the life of the soul, we then have food for nourishing ourselves, and we learn that we can talk back to these core wounds from the inner voice of the soul's personality. None of us escapes the wounding of our limiting environments; we typically land at an adult age realizing that we are not, in fact, acting our chronological age. This is because the wounding we have received along the way has interrupted our evolutionary growth into full maturity and the interruptions along the way have stunted our psychological and spiritual growth. As we offer tolerance, love, and understanding from this internal well, there will be "water in the well" to offer to both ourselves and the external world.

In Gestalt theory/therapy, we speak of building "internal supports" as a foundation to support the "ground of authentic being." Like a tree planted with deep, solid roots, we are free to grow and emerge toward the sky, allowing our branches to expand and reach in all directions. Having a rich inner life means that our internal world feeds us with positive and supportive messages that we can call upon for sustenance on our journey. If our inner life is blocked or full of anxiety and pain, we find ourselves shut down to life, our heart is stone cold. In this constricted, soulless state, we are prone to use an addiction to cover or veil the pain and the fear. Learning to breathe, however simple as that sounds, is a powerful tool in accepting the circumstances in which we find ourselves. As we learn to come into our breath, we begin to honor the *inhale* and the *exhale*, the *contraction* and the *expansion* of life. Respecting the breath of life teaches us to value the movement between *receiving* and *giving*, taking in and moving out while honoring the spaces, pauses, and withdrawals in between.

The illustration on page 81 shows what can occur when the mental effort and concentrated imagining focus on reprogramming negative emotions and destructive affect states with positive emotions and healing images while one is in a shamanic state of consciousness. This graphic displays the energy movement, which is circular for each chakra (about the size of a grapefruit), pictured in the inner vision of the body's container. The healing energy of the infinity symbol expands out in ever-widening circles, traveling beyond the boundaries of the skin and the auric field.

To connect with our souls, *we must learn to balance the energies of the universe within the energy of our bodies*: Earth. Water. Fire. Air. Ether. Ether is the soul of the cosmos, the source of all creation. Ether, as Jung says, is "the *quinta essential* that holds all things together."[1] As we begin to experience this integrative ether energy in our bodies, we can get better at harnessing its healing powers of wholism. In his writing, John Philip Newell discusses the ether element (which he calls "quintus"), which

The Mystical Path: Ecstatic Union + Eroticism (power, love & creativity)
= Embodied Enlightenment

holds in harmony the four elements—earth, air, fire, and water—that constitute the body of the universe.[2] Like systems theory's whole that is greater than or different from the sum of its parts, the image of the Holy is reflected in the unified ether element. Some refer to this as spaciousness or Infinity; others, as God; some, Source; others Soul. This is the face of many faces, the name among many names. Just as with Isis, who was referred to as "the Lady of Ten Thousand Names," we realize that when we come face to face with Holy Mystery, names, descriptions, and language often elude us.

In this human experiment called "life," it is not uncommon to find ourselves flowing between balance and imbalance as we struggle to support life (versus death) energies/realities. It is quite normal to move between the two, but in our core we all know what it feels like to be alive and feel connected to our spontaneous, authentic selves. The key is that we have the skill set to discern (between role versus true nature), to be able to retrieve balance through the awareness of imbalance, life through the awareness of death or dullness. As we open into the tight spaces in our bodies or the anxious knots of constriction, we begin to become aware, without judgment, of when we are in the flow and when we are not; the distinction of fluid versus stuck becomes more apparent. We begin to have awareness of the way in which we can hold these polarities of balance/imbalance, fear/courage, trust/distrust, worry/peace, and we employ the infinity symbol of movement and transformation to shift the immobilizations. As we learn to support the choice of our compassionate, constructive experience, we begin to feel more positive control for managing these containers we call our bodies while nurturing constructive states of stability versus destructive states of instability. We are able to offer ourselves more agency and management, not only in regulating our emotions but also in increasing the stability of our thoughts. As we focus, very simply, on our breath and the elements in nature, we come home to an eternal, primordial state called "soul," and we begin the daily practice of nurturing this aspect of ourselves, fostering a stability of mood, an inner peace, and a state of unconditional love for self and others.

In working with my model of self-perception as "the Tree of Life," we combine shamanistic methodology with elemental breath work in these bodies. This visual construct allows us to assert greater constructive power over the energy fields allowed to exist in our bodies. We learn to exercise

Tree of Life Diagram

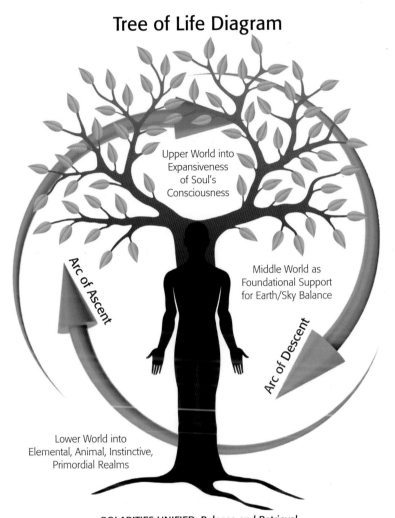

Upper World into
Expansiveness
of Soul's
Consciousness

Middle World as
Foundational Support
for Earth/Sky Balance

Arc of Ascent

Arc of Descent

Lower World into
Elemental, Animal, Instinctive,
Primordial Realms

POLARITIES UNIFIED: Release and Retrieval
Experience of Remembering what the River of Forgetfulness
wants us to forget — Our Soul's Consciousness

choice, distinguishing between the energy fields in the environment that we want to connect with (those that foster constructive interconnection) and those that we don't want to connect with (energies that foster our disconnection and detachment); in psychological terminology, we call this exercising "positive power of control and agency." The field of psychology also utilizes the term "boundary management," distinguishing between permeable and impermeable boundaries. Imagine yourself like a vibrant cell, with permeable, impermeable and semi-permeable boundaries, a living organism with fluid movement toward contact and withdrawal. As we learn the ebb and flow of what we allow in and keep out, we become aware of energies that feed our aliveness and those that do not. Working with our energetic body, experiencing ourselves as trees comforts us by helping us feel rooted in the earth and providing a sense of belonging in this human experience, at the same time reminding us to remain open to the divine realms, the heavens, ether. This is the spiritual world of the Soul Realm, where we will receive wiser information from the higher wisdom mind, which can be decoded and internalized in the human experience in a manner that is grounded, clear, and spiritually practical.

With my embodied Tree of Life construct (which connects us to the larger cosmos), we learn to work in our ever-present bodies with our hands, our mouth, our feet, and our crown, asking the question: *Which do I feed?* The right hand represents the history of chronological wounding that has informed our human personality, and the left hand, over the heart, reminds us of our ability to choose *love*—the divine personality's response—a choice perhaps much different than we might make from our limitations and pain. The mouth in the middle asks: Which do I feed? That which is human? Or that which is Divine? *We are embodied to be enlightened, to be empowered in love.* This is the mantra we can repeat daily as we begin to live at home in our body and make good choices that feed our stability in the world and safety in the container of our body. Like the trees, we are rooted in both stillness and movement, ease and effort, as we align with our soul to fulfill its destiny in the world.

ANALOGY OF THE OPEN PALM VS. THE TIGHT FIST

As we learn to breathe with conscious awareness, we begin to become more aware of the places in our body where our breath is constricted—where we are holding tension and tightness, which is reflective of the places we are locked down to, holding on without consideration of letting go and closed so that, yet again, our hearts cannot remain open to unconditional love. I like to think of our inner constriction as an image of the tight fist. When we encounter our own constriction with compassion, we breathe our breath, with greater awareness, into the constriction, offering openness and receptivity through the inhale breath—through the healing medicine of the open palm (as seen in the inner vision).

Daily Exercise as "Tree of Life" for Active Meditation

Thou kneadest my clay, I know, to make a new universe.

Hazrat Inayat Khan

It is essential to find a sacred space in nature that you can call your own. Allow yourself to connect with a particular spot that nurtures you and fosters a feeling of connectivity with nature and the elements: earth, water, fire, air, and ether. As you become more conscious of the collective powers that exist for you in nature and the direct revelation that awaits you through natural visitations from nature and the animals, you will begin to foster an inner trust and belief in this spiritual practice. Particular messages will be transmitted through your soul's intelligence as you learn how to listen and interpret what is being said. My sacred spot is from my youth, the jetties on the Fort Lauderdale beach near Port Everglades. Each weekend, I would plant myself on these powerful rocks, basking in the sun with the waves of the sea crashing against the rocks, remembering how consistent nature was. The sun always rose. The sun always set. The waves consistently met the shore then fluidly travelled back out to the vast blue sea. There is so much information that flows when we allow ourselves to quiet and merge with nature.

Take a few minutes right now and allow yourself to remember special experiences you had in nature as a younger child or adolescent. Support yourself in remembering where your special places were and what exactly spoke to you about this place. Growing up in Fort Lauderdale, Florida, on a canal that led to the Atlantic Ocean, as a young girl I spent every weekend and many days after school on the water. I had my little eight-foot fiberglass boat with a six-horsepower Mercury engine. I lived freely amongst the five elements without consciously recognizing how profoundly I was affected by their beauty. I was known throughout the neighborhood as the "duck doctor," as I was constantly rescuing the Muscovy ducks from the alligators and manatees that swam down our canal.* As I look back now, I realize that nature and the elements were my salvation—this was my initiation into indigenous wisdom at a very young age—as these beings dialogued daily with me in a very natural way. At the end of my canal, the Jungle Queen riverboat docked, bringing tourists to visit the Native American, first peoples tribes who sold their wares and, with tourists gawking, wrestled alligators to survive. I remember being aware of the obvious distinctions between the natural world and the unnatural and how different the two felt, energetically.

Using elemental breath-work techniques now, as an adult, seems so natural and organic to me (and my clients), conjuring up many wonderful childhood memories for so many. Most of us, as children, felt connected to the woods or the water or the forest. Many adults admit that, when they were children, they found solid comfort and invisible playmate connections in the world of magic and the elements. Many clients report how transformative yet simple this breath work truly is, reconnecting them with the innocence and purity of their younger, more childlike selves. These younger aspects of our adult selves are the aspects that understand the magico-mystical realities of the Soul Realm. Through teaching conscious and deliberate elemental breath work to many clients, I became awakened to deeper imagery and understanding of the Tree of Life. The trees remind us as humans that we need to ground in the earth element while also remaining open to the expansive sky (air and ether elements), bridging the two in these physical bodies, with the trunk of our core and our backbone strong. The Tree of Life imagery is present in Sufism, Native American Spirituality, and many

---

* Interesting note: Ducks as a power animal totem represent emotional comfort and protection.

global mystical traditions, reminding us of the union of stillness and movement. In shamanism and many indigenous societies, it is often through the great World Tree that we journey through the arc of descent into the lower world or into the upper world through the arc of ascent, communication opening, in these physical bodies, between the cosmic planes of earth and heaven. Ontological passage from one mode of being to another (earth, heaven) is possible as the tree becomes the fixed point that renders orientation possible. A center in the chaos is made possible through the tree as we receive guidance, blessings, and ecstatic experience in the upper world and journey into the lower world to retrieve and integrate our lost fragments of soul. This process of ascending and descending is a universal and natural experience, opening the threshold for the shedding of the illusive layers of the false self while holding the truth of who we are in the bones and the bark.

CASE STUDY: GERTRUDE'S BREAKTHROUGH

Gertrude is a client who was working to stand up and speak her truth to her husband. In a therapeutic session, she conveyed that it was important to her that she own her truth in all its fullness and softness while understanding his point of view as well. We did elemental breaths together before drumming, and she suddenly exclaimed, "I feel as though I have found my backbone. I need to push back against him. I think he actually likes it when I do that." Through grounding and centering with the medicine of the elements, Gertrude encountered greater personal power and clarity of truth. As she practiced doing this in daily life with her husband, their relationship shifted into a richer experience of shared power and mutually respectful understanding. Learning to feel our spine supporting our back body helps us support the front body, creating open space in the heart and the lungs. As we become aware of the way in which our backbone holds us up, we find it easier to breathe and feel support from the inside. As you play with the experiment of experiencing your inner trunk, ask yourself the question, *What sources my creative impulse to breathe?* Where does this urge to breathe come from? And what can I do daily to foster my own deepened connection with my sacred breath? Clients repeatedly report how liberating it is to live in their bodies in a more relaxed way, simply through conscious breath.

CENTERING EXERCISE: GROUND IN EARTH
AS A SUPPORTIVE, HOLDING EMBRACE

As we begin a daily centering practice, it is best to start with the root, the earth element. We place the soles of our feet firmly on the earth—all four corners of each foot—coming into an experience of "I am Here; I Belong." The root chakra is the energy center where trust versus fear is internally negotiated. The earth breath is through the nose—the inhale and exhale breaths, both through the nose. This helps bring our breath into our sacrum, our hips, our base; from there we move the breath down our legs, into our feet, filling even our toes with both rootedness and spaciousness. This experience of embodying into our soles helps us to reach up into the realm of Soul, from *sole to soul*. Again, this kundalini energy is the sacred fire found in the base of the spine, in your sacrum (where the "dragon tail" resides). When it rises from the base of the spine to the crown of the head, it quickens and awakens and clears blocked energies in the internal energetic body. Often the serpent will be seen through the eyes of inner vision or can be visualized unwrapping and unraveling as it travels with its medicine up the spine, bringing us its life-sustaining, awakening energies with greater strength of flexible backbone.

We move next into the belly, the water element, the sacral chakra, the place of the womb, where the medicinal emotional waters that feed birthing, rebirthing, and creativity dwell. This is the belly of desire, where affect states, including guilt, are contained, embraced, and sorted. Feelings often gestate way beyond their time in this energy space, and we need to learn the skill of holding on long enough to create awareness while practicing surrender and letting go—so that our inner energy fields are not blocked or immobilized. The water breath helps us relax into letting go and "giving to the river" as we breathe in through the nose and out through the mouth. It is helpful to imagine a waterfall above your head, moving in through the crown and clearing out that which must go, as you exhale through the mouth. Eventually, as you keep breathing into this water breath, you will begin to flow internally with the rhythm of water, merging with a wave-like movement, perhaps experiencing the translucent powers of purifying, cleansing water. As you merge with the water element, you will begin to feel more fluid in your body and find yourself opening to imagery of letting go and surrendering with greater ease.

Next we move to the solar plexus, the third chakra, the fire element, the space of sun consciousness. This is the place of the will; the primary focus in this energy center is personal power and the ability to act courageously from our center. Shame and anxiety are often lodged in this space, blocking our ability to access our personal power and will power. The tight fist felt in this area will block one's ability to access one's personal power. The fire element breath is in through the mouth, out through the nose. Often the inner vision may see a flame, like a burning candle, or perhaps a dragon with a flame of fire. It is essential to harness the fire element and create balance with the earth and water elements, to begin to experience these different elements in balance in the internal space of the body's container. As we learn to experience this internal space in our body and create breath in the solar plexus, we will experience a return to personal power, greater clarity, and alignment of will into action. These are the aligned energies of a sun consciousness within one's body.

In every color (of our colorful inner energy system) there is the light. This light brings greater vibrancy to each color, and its vibrational essence moves into the foreground as we work to release unwanted wounded energies and retrieve the constructive energies of light and love. In every stone sleeps a crystal, again reminding us of the earth-sky interconnection and the light that always waits to transform the darkness. Once these energies of earth, water, and fire are connected and aligned internally—again, working always from the inside out—we begin to experience an interconnectedness with all living things. As we first ground in the earth while still connecting deeply to the sky, we can move more freely into the center of our being (which is light and love, the expanded heart). This movement inward is the awakening of the heart space, the air element. We integrate a sun consciousness with a moon consciousness—masculine and feminine energies harnessed and balanced in the spaciousness of the chest. Imagine a whole, open heart with flames burning both for you and for the world. Some like to imagine the heart lifting and expanding in the center of the heart space cavity like an umbrella, opening the throat: our ability to share publicly that which is private—to bring our authentic selves out into the world.

The fourth chakra, the heart space, the air element, is the central space, embracing unconditional love (which can only be divinely inspired).

The air breath is accessed by breathing in through the mouth and out through the mouth, which opens the throat, the portal of connection between the mind and the heart. Feel free to make lots of noise now with your breath; even coughing may often overtake you as you are clearing inner energy fields. You will begin to feel more space opening around your heart, as if weighty puzzle pieces are falling off your shoulders, being permanently transfigured by earth, water, fire, and air medicine. The weight of the world will drop as the heart feels more open, perhaps lighter and more expansive. The heart space is where we receive and give love. When we feel a tightening around our heart and our clavicle area, tension results and we experience ourselves as closed to the outside world (as well as to our inner truth). Many different spiritual traditions speak of the heart as the "secret chamber," the inner altar and meditation room where we deepen our connection with unconditional love. The heart chakra is typically referred to as the "mystical, sacred space," or the "inner altar," or the "garden of light," even the "inner cave," where the potential for powerful transformation resides. Different spiritual traditions speak of the three flames: 1) power, 2) wisdom, and 3) love. All three coalesce in this space of sun-moon consciousness intertwined. When we seek to open this space, we are seeking to melt the hardness of heart or mend the unmerciful heart that may exist due to the wounding of life experiences. This space can hold grief and relationship issues and needs moon consciousness to soften the rough edges and deepen into the wisdom of inner vision, understanding, and compassion.

Many of my clients have seen images of their inner heart like a cinder block or steel. This is symbolic of the ways in which the heart space holds on to pain, grief, and suffering and imagines that it is protecting us by closing off our hearts from the world. It is helpful to practice daily activities that awaken the cultivation of an open, expansive heart. The mind and the heart seek to function in a unified manner within the body. The throat is the bridge of connection between the two, from air to ether, open space infused by Spirit. The heart reference is not to the physical organ of the heart but rather to the spiritual center, where we are rooted in giving and receiving love. The heart—the core of our being—must be open in order for Divine Love to flow through us. Our journey is about internal interactive embodiment, informed by a practice that helps us stay open rather than closed.

The fifth chakra, the throat space, connects air to ether. It too is awakened by breathing in through the mouth and out through the mouth. As you practice this breath in the back of your throat, imagine your throat widening, making space for a wider bridge of connection between your heart and your head. If the throat is tight or closed, the energy will not flow freely, and it will be difficult to speak up in your life from a place of clear connection between your head and your heart. This separation may make for bad decisions, especially when it comes to relationship and love matters. Opening the throat chakra is about speaking truth; the sixth chakra is about seeing truth; and the seventh chakra is about knowing truth. As we open to this ethereal alignment in the crown of our head, we will see into the Divine Realm and will learn to listen to the voice of Wisdom, also known as "Sophia" energies. We begin to learn how to harness these powers and embody them, applying this knowledge practically to the way we live our daily lives. Sometimes, you may see a third eye in this space of the throat, opening wide and connecting with the third eye of inner vision in the sixth chakra.

The sixth and seventh chakras are also about opening further to the ether element, breathing in through the nose and out through the nose, while experiencing the return to the earth and the connection beyond the earth realm, simultaneously. The etheric plane is believed to be the highest plane in matter. It is as real as the physical plane but exists in higher dimensions of consciousness. It is believed in many spiritual traditions that *the Etheric Realm houses the blueprint of your divine plan.* All the memories of your soul are believed to be stored here, including the memories of this and all lifetimes. This ethereal realm is more easily accessed in shamanic states of consciousness, with the aid of the beat of the frame drum or other meditative states.[3]

In shamanic methodology, we speak of the upper world, the middle world, and the lower world. The concept, briefly described, is that the Soul Realm—this hidden universe—is an *integrated and inclusive* reality eager and waiting to help us on this human journey. We merely need to *ask for practical wisdom and guidance, so that the hidden realities will be revealed to us.* In a similar vein, consistent with the soul's consciousness, Jesus also told us to "knock, and the door shall be opened" (Matthew 7:7). In this middle world, as humans, our bodies embody past incarnations of our soul. As a result of doing this work, the more we uncover our soul's enduring themes, the more our lives begin to fall into place and make more sense as the soul perspective sheds light on the human reality, helping us minimize reactivity and engage the wise mind's response.

The divine beings in the unseen universe, in both the upper world and the lower world, are powerful ones who are not affiliated with a religion; they work to assist humankind in all wholesome endeavors. Depending on which faith tradition you draw from, you may speak of gods, goddesses, mythic heroes, nature spirits, elementals—the whimsical faery creatures of folktales and dreams—sorcerers, shamans, or power animals. Our job is to learn how to dialogue with these soul beings directly, without need for outside representation or mediation. While this can be a bit daunting in the beginning, like any relationship, the more we deepen the conversation, the more we learn and are comforted in the exchange. Basic communication involves both listening and speaking. *The same is true in soul-retrieval practice.* While it is essential to come with our intention and to ask the Soul Realm for what we believe we need, we must also stay open and listen to what our soul tells us. It is our soul that is the best listener to the voice of the Soul Realm. Our mind and busy brain are often preoccupied with analyzing what is going on, but *our soul knows exactly how to interpret the voice of Mystery.* When we don't censor or second-guess ourselves, our soul knows immediately what means what. We want to practice openness and call in all our soul helpers, those in both the lower world and the upper world. These beings have been referred to by many different names, met throughout the ages, on many diverse continents, by many on mystical journeys through numerous landscapes.

In shamanic methodology, the upper world is often greeted by the Ascended Masters, perhaps Mother Mary, Jesus, the Buddha, the archangels, the crone (or hag woman), the sages, the warriors, the magicians, the gods and goddesses, and many divine beings, some who remain faceless and nameless for quite some time. These are believed to be the creatures who have incarnated, lived this human experience in this earthly realm, and have now ascended into greater, enlightened states. It is uncanny how I have seen a certain figure when in a shamanic state (in the Soul Realm) and then months, even years later, learning and researching a name, found that the image I saw while in a shamanic state is consistent with the image recorded by others.

The lower world, in shamanic methodology, is full of the elementals: the hidden peoples; the nature spirits; the creatures of earth, air, fire, and water. Those who serve the earth element are often called gnomes. Those who serve the air element are referred to as sylphs. Those who serve the fire element are called salamanders. Those who serve the water element are referred to as the undines. The fairies, sprites, and leprechauns (the forest folk), which Celtic shamanism discusses at length, are deeply committed to lightness and play and long for our reunion with our child-like, spontaneous selves. These beings often appear in the lower world, bringing joy to our spirits and elevation to our souls, which are often found stuck at the bottom of the sea or buried deep down in the belly of the earth. Know that these soul beings are always deeply committed to our enlightenment, our soul's ascension.

As we begin to understand the fluidity of the shamanic model, the release and retrieval, we open more deeply to valuing the life force of soul vibration. Our breath, the animating force of all life, expands and contracts with less interruption. On good days, we even begin to feel as though our breath flows with the fullness of the moon. We begin to understand that the Soul Realm will freely offer its medicine, its balm, always awaiting our visit. As we deepen in dialogue with the beings of the Soul Realm—the Creator, the Preserver, the Destroyer, the Regenerator—we grow in wisdom and gain an appreciation for the life/death/rebirth cycle of all of life. As we live attached to our souls, embodied, we realize that through extraction work we can release the unwanted introjects of the wounded environmental field that we have internalized, believing them to be our true self when, in fact, they are not.

NAMASTE TO MISS LUCKY

On a moist, early May morning I did my ritual approach to the chicken coop with food and water for my girls. There was a smell of death in the air. Then I saw my favorite Rhode Island Red hen, Miss Lucky, quietly sitting in the corner of an aluminum coop that hadn't been used for years. This was very unlike her, and I wondered how she had managed to squeeze herself through the quarter-inch space of an opening. Her squeezing through that tiny space, the "eye of a needle," still remains a mystery to me. Miss Lucky, who had been named by my youngest son when she was just a newborn chick—"just because," he had said at five and a half—was the one who laid the golden eggs (only hers were a turquoise blue). She had lived happily, way beyond her years, at least eleven (which is a lot in chicken years). This morning I found her all alone, in the corner. She had safely sequestered herself from the three other hens, knowing she was dying. What was it that had caused her to separate herself? Was this instinct or animal intelligence or the soul's awareness of death? Upon closer examination, I saw that the other three hens were carefully witnessing this process, as if they knew something as well and were very much *with her* in it. Sacred chicken knowledge about life and death, communicated back and forth?

As I sat with them, I realized this is the way in which our souls witness our human journey. *It's as if they watch us through our many life/ death incarnations.* Our souls witness the way in which we humans get all worked up about such secular stuff—the profane world—forgetting our divine origins and our soul's seed of memory. Musing, I imagined our souls cheering for us, saying, *"Stay on track," "Follow the star," "Listen to that inner voice, it's me," "You can reach your destiny; we need you to."* The next morning, May 7, Miss Lucky had passed, seemingly brave and knowing.

This cycle we witness in nature begins to make sense in the patterns of our lives, through the lens of soul. We practice releasing the imprint of our wounded selves as we open to the retrieval of a new understanding of who we truly are, as redefined through the eyes of Soul.

GROWING FROM THE INSIDE OUT

In closing chapter 4, repeat the elemental mantra below as a way of invoking the sentiments of the Serenity Prayer combined with a desire to embody greater balance. After repeating the words, practice each elemental breath. As you learn to comfortably inhale and exhale while making noise and sounds, inhale again, *pause* (holding the breath), and exhale. In this simple act, you will experience your body deepening into greater balance and will feel more rooted and grounded, in an embodied way. It is essential that we ground and experience our bodies first before moving into meditative/shamanic states. We want to always ground the spiritual experience in these physical bodies, which is why we begin with the earth breath. Remember, allow yourself to make noise with your breath. You may even need to cough. You can even begin by plugging each ear with an index finger to deepen into the sound of your own breath, like an ocean wave. Once you experience yourself deepening into the sound of your own breath, you can remove your fingers. As you embody each element in your body and imagine each element balancing itself with the others, you will begin to feel different sensations in your body. Take time to notice what you feel. Most likely, you will be calibrated to a higher vibration through this exercise. Allow the experience to bring you calm and to center you in your being.

THE DAILY ELEMENTAL MANTRA

To be practiced anywhere and everywhere, throughout your day, while imagining yourself like a tree:

Power of Earth: Root me in truth. Like a tree trunk, ground me in my soul's knowledge.

Earth Breath: In through the nose, out through the nose.

Power of Water: Flow through me with ease and grace, to embrace that which I cannot change—that which is my soul's destiny.

Water Breath: In through the nose, out through the mouth.

Power of Fire: Infuse me with your strength, power, and courage to change the things I can through the power of my will and your will aligned.

Fire Breath: In through the mouth, out through the nose.

Power of Air: Open me to your inspiration and vision as I traverse the two worlds through my wise inner knowing, accepting those things that I cannot change.

Air Breath: In through the mouth, out through the mouth.

Power of Ether: Fill me with an attachment to you through the circular inhale and exhale of each full-moon breath, that I may live as One with all living beings.

Ether breath returns as in the cycle of life to the **Earth Breath:** In through the nose, out through the nose.

CHAPTER 5

THE CALLING OUT:
THE INCANTATION OF SOUL

> *The only true wisdom is in knowing you know nothing . . .*
> *for I know one thing, and that is that I know nothing.*
>
> SOCRATES

THE ETHEREAL WORLD: THE SOUL'S INTELLIGENCE

In the ethereal realm—the mystical realm encompassing but not limited to the medicine of earth, water, fire, air, and ether—our souls are rooted in the knowledge of their destiny throughout the enduringness of all time: past, present, and future. Time runs together for soul; truly one day is like a thousand years. When we are connected to the world of Infinity through our souls, we will not be fully at home in this physical plane, the middle world of linear time. The irony of our human existence in this middle world is that our souls desperately seek to grow and expand into their fullness through this physical human reality while, at the same time, they long to be "unstained by the world" (James 1:27). Somehow, while embodying purity of soul, our souls seek a daily human existence embedded in a world that is contrary to the world of Soul. As we await and ready ourselves for our soul's unraveling, moment by moment, everywhere in life, we learn that we have only to remain open to Spirit—to have eyes to see and ears to hear. Spiritual meditation and practice is not a time that we set aside from the rest of our day, but a time to practice union with our very souls, throughout daily life. Moment-to-moment daily living becomes an active, moving meditation. In nature, the signs are everywhere: the crow's "caw, caw" speaks to us as we open our door in the morning and catch ourselves pausing to listen. In these mystical moments we can be reminded that our soul is with us, and we practice remaining open to our soul's unfolding, listening trustingly to whatever messages come through from the Soul Realm.

Spirituality is often viewed as an individual's search for the Divine, not as the Divine's search for the individual. The illusion nurtured through this perception is that soul-to-Soul is a one-way relationship. Too little is discussed about the way in which we are pursued—expressing Holy Mystery's desire to know and be known. As is true in all relationships, there is an exchange. The reciprocity of back-and-forth dialogue deepens the relationship—building trust, familiarity, ease, and desire for closeness of connection. It is no different with the Soul Realm and our own souls. As we learn to make noise so that we are heard, and we tug and shout and persist in speaking out, we are responded to in kind. This is why, in the shamanic tradition, we drum, we chant, we rattle, we dance, we clap; we make noise to awaken this hidden universe, as if saying to the spirits, "I am here. Humbly, respond."

Over the years, I have worked with so many clients who have been steeped in a sinner self-perception due to destructive religious dogma's early imprint. This "programming" makes it difficult to trust that the Soul Realm, which is seemingly unknowable to a "sinner," eagerly awaits their communion. In addition, due to the betrayals and disappointments of life, many clients arrive at my office shut down and frozen in their hearts, not willing to trust or believe that anything really matters. In spiritual terminology, this is called "a crisis of hope." In Gestalt psychological terminology, we speak of this as "existential despair." Either way, this is a crippling affect state that locks the body in a state of constriction. Once we allow this tiny seed of memory to awaken within, we reawaken to hope renewed, discovering that we can begin to believe again. We come to realize that, in spite of our wounded, imperfect imprint, we remain the "beloved," cared for like the tiny sparrow. Believing "each hair on our head is numbered," meaning that we are very intimately known by our Creator, we then can move into the realization of who we truly are through our soul's lens of perception. Through this soul awareness, seeing who we truly are in beauty, truth, and purity, we become our inner landscape. If we are not able to experience ourselves as beloved, loved by God (from the inside out), then the pursuit of the Soul Realm will be futile, confirming our skewed sinner mentality. Our inner beliefs will house the wounded core of skepticism, distrust, unworthiness, and disbelief, telling us that we carry minimal value or worth. The task of encountering and even dialoguing with Divine Mystery will appear so overwhelming and daunting that we will stop ourselves or distract ourselves from receiving this healing medicine before we even get started.

According to psychological theory, one of the primary needs of the human is to know and be known. We must remind ourselves that it is the same with Divine Mystery. Our soul is very eager to be known by us so that we can incorporate its sacred information into our daily living. Unfortunately, many world religions, with their narrow prescriptions, have fallen short in guiding us to access a deepened soul experience, which can be understood only through an expanded state of consciousness. Religious dogma, with its constricted philosophies, shuts down the portal into expanded perception. It was Plato who said, "And what, Socrates, is food for the soul?" With Socrates replying, "Surely, I said, Knowledge is food for the soul."[1] What exactly is this particular *knowledge* that the soul seeks, and how do we better access it? This is the pursuit we will continually make as we practice soul journeying in shamanic states.

CASE STUDY: MARY BETH'S EPIPHANY

The power of this work is palpable in the case of Mary Beth, a mid-life woman who came to me with the goal of understanding why she repeatedly ended up in relationships with men who, she reported, "expressed the shadow side, aka the darker energies," which she found so repugnant. Her history included multiple stories of men who were abusive, both verbally and physically, and she carried lots of shame about the fact that she repeatedly found herself in these sorts of relationships. Mary Beth was working to understand why she continued to repeat this destructive habitual pattern and sought healing in breaking it. As we worked both on a psychological level and with the shamanic process, she realized that her worldview of darkness and light was not an integrated one. She began to see that her perspective was quite divided, in what represented a body split, a dichotomy of perception and being.

As we moved closer to uncovering the blockages in her own body, her heart began to race and she felt palpitations. When she brought her own hand to her heart and made safe contact with herself, she began to focus on bringing her breath into her heart. Inner self-dialogue was also helpful as she told herself, "I am ready now to face this. I can bravely look into my relationship with myself to better understand how I am acting out my own woundedness in my relationships with men." Mary Beth realized that she held a dualistic view that was quite fragmented. She perceived herself as a "person of light," a healer herself, and these men she dated, the shadow. They were the ones who carried the darkness, not her. As we worked together, she was drawn outside the windows of my office to observe the clouds. It was a rainy, misty day and she was taken by how the dark clouds moved into the blue sky and then were overtaken by the light of the sun. Eventually, she realized that the dark and the light were in a constant flow, with light moving into dark and dark moving into the light. She began to understand the possibility of a more integrated model of light and dark in fluid contact with each other, as if a continuum of movement was more the norm. She understood that she needed to face the shadow side of herself—her own violent urges, her aggression, her anger—and she began to understand that what was unfolding in nature outside her was the mirror image of her interiority. As Mary Beth embraced these disowned aspects of herself and used her inhale and exhale breaths to move into deeper awareness, embracing compassionate acceptance, she moved into a state of peace, realizing that if she could own and embrace her anger and aggression, she would actually move into her own power more fully. Her "warrior self" emerged to explain to her that these worlds needed to be seen as two aspects of the whole: an interior that she could allow herself to embrace in all its aspects, supporting herself to emerge toward greater wholeness of darkness and light within her own being. She understood that once she accepted this as occurring within herself, she would no longer seek the external environmental experience to repeatedly offer her this insight.

Mary Beth discovered that she needed to embrace her anger and aggression as "beautiful" and own her voice more fully, setting greater limits with others about what was tolerable and what was unacceptable. As my yoga teacher often affirms, "*the fastest way to freedom is to feel.*" As Mary Beth practiced embracing her own true emotion, radical acceptance of her human emotional state without judgment and shame allowed her to leave the session experiencing herself as more whole. This is because she was able to fully embrace both shadow and light while still opening to the light as healing medicine. This realization enabled her to shed greater compassion on the darker, more wounded, disowned aspects of her being, bringing about a huge shift in her life (as she reported in later sessions). Again, this is an example of the release-and-retrieval method of shamanic methodology as outlined in this book.

After this session I realized that, as we drummed together and she called in her soul protectors and her helping spirits, wisdom and insight were called in in a way that I might never have imagined or suggested as her psychotherapist. The intervention that was necessary for the next stage of her evolutionary growth was exactly what her soul knew. Her soul's knowing was specific to what was needed for her to be able to digest the higher consciousness information, the medicine necessary for the next stages of her growth, in a practical way, drawing easily from nature. This is a good time to remind us all that *our soul always knows exactly what is needed for the next incremental step in its ascension.* In this case, awareness of sensation, the tightness and blockage Mary Beth initially felt in her heart, became the gateway into the deeper expression of her soul's voice. As we pay attention to the tight spots, where the tension lives in our body, we often find the place of sensation that opens up the portal into our soul's clarity. This clarity will unfold moment by moment, step by step if we practice staying open. In this practice, we learn to trust that a "spoonful of medicine" is given to us as we allow ourselves to receive healing and insight, one spoonful at a time.

CALLING IN THE SPIRITS TO LIFT THE VEIL

Staying open and mindful to "knowing what we don't know that we don't know" is no small task; it is also a central theme of this book. This may sound baffling—but think about it. When we remember to remain humble and open about what we think we know for certain, we suspend our certainty and acknowledge that there may be more wisdom about another reality unfolding than we are aware of at this point in time. This is the experience of remaining receptive and available to the Divine while still being rooted in something foundational, which is what we are comfortable with in our human flesh. Knowledge is a tricky phenomenon, often causing us to shut down because we think we know for certain what we believe we know. If we stay open in our minds to Mystery, to sacred knowledge—phenomenologically shaped by repeated experience—we will be transformed by the discovery of a new layer of practical, valuable information.

"Gnosis" is the Greek word used to describe this sort of knowledge—a type of knowledge, derived from experience, that encompasses the whole of a person and potentially effects change in a more embodied or holistic manner than does cognition alone. Gnosis is what you will receive as you remain persistent in dialoguing with the Soul Realm. It may be "divination" you seek—meaning help in problem solving—or meaningful guidance or answers to specific questions. Or it may be comfort and support from the Soul Realm, offering you strength, courage, and insight into your daily life. Or perhaps you may seek to learn more about the secret knowledge that various spiritual traditions have taught their students throughout the ages. This shamanic meditative practice suggests that you work straight with Source in seeking transcendence to find your answers.

As you call out into the Soul Realm, you will begin to have an experience of the veil being lifted and you will begin to see with your seer sight. Even if you frame this in Jungian psychological terms of "the collective unconscious material" or you see this as an aspect of the imaginal realm dancing with your imagination, I ask that you simply remain open and receptive to the information as it comes. From a shamanic worldview, you may begin to ponder the idea that it is your own soul offering direct revelation of its knowledge to you. As you have repeated experiences, you will learn to trust and act upon this information as an aspect of your own expanded intelligence. The more you allow yourself to do this, the more gnosis will take root in your being, having a positive effect on your healing, wholeness, and maturation into greater wisdom.

In meditative and shamanic states of consciousness, we are able to look face-to-face and see the "faceless ones" as they willingly reveal themselves to us, one small image at a time. In ancient stories of mythology, there are countless depictions of the gods and goddesses hiding and then revealing their faces. Even in the Bible, the face of God was hidden from view in the Old Testament. Yet Exodus 3:2 reads, "And the angel of the Lord appeared to Moses in a blazing fire from the midst of a bush;

and he looked, and behold, the bush was burning with fire, yet the bush was not consumed." It is very common in various spiritual traditions for divine deities to morph and move, as if playing a game of hide-and-seek with our expectations and perceptions. It is in the New Testament, with the incarnation of Jesus as "the Son of God, the Light of the World," that we are given a face with characteristic remnants of the ancient sun gods and goddesses that the generations before had worshipped.

When we see the inner light, through the third eye, it often appears in a circle, like the golden sun or the warmth of the full moon lit brightly in the night sky. Often, many other colors of the rainbow will encircle this light as well, usually effecting healing in our internal structure and/ or energy centers. Once you experience this, allow your inner body to receive this healing and begin to allow the internal spiral to move outward. You may even feel drawn to bring your loved ones into this circle of light and love and then extend this beautiful, peaceful energy out into the global world.

THE FACES OF GODS AND GODDESSES

The Druidic religion is one among many world mythologies (particularly traditions integrating nature) that contain teachings about a mother goddess and powerful female deities who occasionally showed their faces to the faithful. Knowing the secret name of a deity was believed to enable one to have the power of that deity, so names and/or faces were magical gifts bestowed from above. Understandably, seeing the face of a deity was even more profound than knowing the name alone. Names have been used to implore a deity to reveal his or her face and mysteriously bestow the deity's powerful medicine.

In Egyptian mythology, Isis was known as "the Lady of Ten Thousand Names" and was revered above all. The belief in her protective powers and magical potions was central to her entire mythology. Invoking the curative powers of the milk of Isis had a central role in Egyptian magical spells and rituals honoring the life/death/rebirth cycles of nature.

In the Catholic tradition, many faithful have confessed to apparitional physical experiences at certain sacred sites around the world, seeing the face of the Ancient Mother, Mother Mary. She is often seen in blue and white robes, surrounded by a great white light.

Appreciating that there are many paths to enlightenment when you are communing in the integrated and inclusive realm of Soul will help you understand the many faces and the many names as they appear. The sphere is indeed an integrated and inclusive community of divine beings eager to be seen and known by their faithful followers—in incremental steps, of course. If you come from a specific spiritual tradition, it is most likely that you will see specific spirit beings from your faith tradition. If you are an atheist or a pagan, you will most likely see imagery and spirit beings that speak directly to your soul. Again, remember, this is not a book about religious dogma. This is a guide to provide phenomenological experience with your own soul. Psychology speaks of our human experience as the desire to know and be known. In the Spirit World, in the land of souls, the desire is to see and be seen. Most spiritual traditions have a ritual for calling in the spirits or calling out to the Soul Realm. It is basically the experience of making noise to get souls' attention and let them know we are here: I am here. This concept is reflected in the words of Jesus, "Seek and ye shall find; knock and the door shall be opened, only ask, and it shall be given" (Matthew 7:7) As we grow into our soul's maturity, we learn that the prayer or mantra "Thy will be done" (Matthew 6:10) paradoxically nestles side by side with intentional requests. This is the magical moment of deep surrender and alignment with the Holy Will.

Eckhart Tolle, in his book *The Power of Now: A Guide to Spiritual Enlightenment*, refers to this as the path of consecrated action.[2] He discusses the need to not be concerned with the fruit of our action but instead to give attention to the action itself. The fruit will come of its own accord. In many different spiritual traditions, this is viewed as a powerful spiritual practice of devotion and service to the Divine; for example, it is discussed in the Bhagavad Gita, where nonattachment to the fruit of your action is called "karma yoga."

THE "I AM SELF" MEETS THE "I AM THAT I AM" OF SOUL

As we stay open to what comes and who comes, we learn *first* to accept the unfolding; *second*, we learn that it is okay to keep asking for more if we remain unclear or uncertain about the information revealed to us. In our humanness, our inner vision may begin to see dimly but perhaps wants or needs more clarity to fully understand. It is important that you not be afraid to ask for more and that you specifically request to be encircled by more powerful spirits. *Imagine that you will be in a circle of protection by enlightened ancestors. Courageous spirit guides. Animal helpers.* You may see wood nymphs, symbolizing the earth element, offering you its medicine, or perhaps the sea nymphs, bringing the medicine of the water element to your being. Each image is a divine spirit animating nature's medicine, coming to offer itself as healing for you. This is basically their "job." This is why they exist, awaiting our call for healing, for aid, for support, for gnosis.

THE SOUL'S SONG

When I drum with my clients, I often observe that each soul is awakened by its own tune or melody, specific to its developmental readiness to reveal itself. It is important that you access your own soul's song. My clients and I now affirm together that we hear a particular tune in the drumbeat, as if the drumbeat is moving up and down the energy centers in the internal body, tuning and attuning where needed. Wherever you are in the life cycle, it is important to remember that your soul knows exactly what you need to perfectly respond to your next level of evolutionary growth or soul's ascension. Your soul will often send you a little melody, offered as medicine, to jump-start and assist. The Soul Realm works with specific vibrational melodies to try to awaken and heal whatever is dormant within. These melodies with specific tonal qualities will often come to you on their own when you are in a meditative state, in close union with your soul. Or, as one client reported, a soul tune came to her when she was in the shower enjoying the water streaming down her body, in a quieter, internal state. As you allow yourself more time for personal reflection, such as meditating with the practices of this book for ten to fifteen minutes in the morning and evening, you will begin to see greater results. Your soul's tune will be self-soothing and will evoke images specific to the healing needs of whatever is troubling you at the time. The power of this music, especially combined with a drumbeat mimicking the beat of the heart, will elevate you to a vibration that stirs awakening of kundalini energy, your own life force, unblocked. As you learn to embrace the mystical life and trust that your soul has its own song, this melody will feed your vitality, personal power, and healing potential so that you can live connected to your soul's vibration, every day. Music and the arts often attach us with our soul's expression if we can only allow ourselves to listen inside, to the yearnings awaiting embodiment.

I recently started working with a new client, Tim, who related that he felt drawn to return to playing the piano and the flute, as he had done when he was a young boy and an adolescent. Yet now, he says quizzically, he finds himself avoiding both. Oddly enough, he just turned fifty and finds himself in an existential crisis, looking for a new career path but facing a blank slate. He reports that his life is good. He has a happy, satisfying marriage; he's raised his three kids and they are well launched, yet he finds himself staying up late at night, thinking a lot about his youthful spirit (which he believes was much more active and alive than his spirit now) while gorging himself on wine and cheese. He has decided he wants to do some work with me and explore the awakening of his soul to see if this might help him somehow.

I later reflected on how much Tim's struggle resonated with me. As a young girl, I too, was trained in classical piano and also played the flute—which brought me neither a feeling of abandonment nor one of liberation. I believe the reason I felt so constrained was that I was trained classically; if my soul had been free to find its own path, I would have been playing rhythm and blues and folk ballads. This is the resistance yet to be embraced, and mine is a common experience that we all must encounter in the practice of staying attuned to our soul's expression and answering back to the resistance. This can serve as a reminder that, when we are in the realm of Soul, we know so because *we find true liberation and abandonment of being, which fosters a feeling of joy, ecstasy, and bliss.* Self-consciousness, a characteristic of reserved interruption, isn't operational when we are in our soul flow. We very simply feel aligned with our true expression, uncensored. Our soul is at home doing what it longs to be doing and we relax into this space with ease of release.

For me, sadly there have been times in my life, in my late twenties and then again in my early forties, when I simply stopped playing the piano and the flute (and, more drastically, stopped listening to my favorite music) after experiencing devastating losses. This is not uncommon. For many of us, after times of significant loss and grief, our spirits despair and we shut down, closing off our hearts. Contracting into rigid constriction, we live in perpetual detachment from our souls. It hurts too much to live life with a whole, open heart. We stop feeding joy because we no longer trust it. Our inner music turns the "off" switch and we stop believing that we can truly be happy. Allowing our muse to die, we stop listening from the inside out, we mute our muse, and eventually the music goes. In Gestalt terminology, we call this the "death layer," which holds the emotional/affect states of hopelessness, despair, powerlessness, and helplessness.

Usually, you will recognize your soul's song as it comes to you naturally, especially if you invite its presence with an open, whole heart. It is not a forced tune that you make up. It comes in an organic, repetitive manner while you are in a meditative, shamanic state with your soul. Once it comes, your soul will immediately recognize it and be comforted—and the song will stick. It will keep coming and you will keep remembering it. The more you meditate, the more the tune will keep returning to you, like a mantra. This is very natural. Do not force it. Trust that it will come, and when it comes, let it know that you recognize it and that you are grateful for its return.

There have been numerous cases, with multiple clients, in which I have heard a song in my inner being, which I start to hum or chant out loud with my client. Immediately, my client recognizes the song as an awakening of his or her heart. My client's soul responds and inner vision and imagery start to abound for them. When these songs come through me, they are designed to specifically awaken both the heart and the soul of my clients. When I hear one of these songs in my inner being, I simply mimic the tune out loud as I hear it and wait to see how my client responds. These are the phenomenological experiments that are so heartening. As we learn to listen inside and trust the organic response, we are given more information as the soul awakens. This is the gnosis I spoke of earlier. If you hear an inner tune or song or chant, simply repeat it and see how your being responds. If the response is favorable, the song is most likely necessary medicine for your soul.

CASE STUDY: MARK—"BUT I AM AFRAID"

I recently had a client, Mark, who explained that he repeatedly felt as if his head was going to "explode" when doing this work on his own, without me in the room. This visceral experience caused him to feel afraid to go deeper into the work on his own (with his soul helpers). Mark reported that he encountered intense excitement while simultaneously feeling nervousness. I explained that his reaction was the normal response—as one learns to shut down the "monkey mind," or busy brain, and begins to experience other aspects of one's being as real. As with Mark, if you feel an anticipation of some sort of internal explosion, do not be afraid to breathe into this and support yourself in moving beyond the constrictions of your limited perceptions. Once you burst through this experience and learn that you can "move to the other side" and be okay, you will gain greater confidence in moving beyond your fears into a surrender to something greater—this is your personal encounter with your expansive self, your soul. Allow yourself this experience just once and you will gain greater confidence and competency to go there on a regular basis. Remember, repeated exposure decreases sensitization. As you allow yourself the repeated experience of this shamanic work, you will become less and less afraid of encountering your soul in such practical ways. You will begin to be comforted by the notion that your soul is your closest ally and spiritual friend, your unconditionally loving Mother/Father/Creator.

NO BEGINNING AND NO END: CALLING IN THE CIRCLE

What then is time? If no one asks me, I know what it is. If I wish to explain it to him who asks, I do not know.

ST. AUGUSTINE

Understanding the life of the soul is much like the experience St. Augustine describes in this quote—you instinctively know when you are accessing its information yet you may not find it so easy to explain it. Parmenides, the shamanic philosopher whom Plato called "father," and the only philosopher he referred to as having depth, believed that time was not real, declaring "nor was it ever, nor will it be, since now it is, altogether one, continuous." Mircea Eliade distinguishes between sacred time and profane duration, comparing the two:

By its very nature sacred time is reversible in the sense that, properly speaking, it is a primordial mythical time made present. Every religious festival, any liturgical time, represents the reactualization of a sacred event that took place in a mythical past, in the beginning. . . . Hence sacred time is indefinitely recoverable, indefinitely repeatable. From one point of view it could be said that it does not pass, that it does not constitute an irreversible duration. It is an ontological, Parmenidean time; it always remains equal to itself, it neither changes nor is exhausted.[3]

Einstein concurred: "For us believing physicists, this separation between past, present, and future is an illusion, however stubborn."[4] Those of us who enter into shamanic states of consciousness know this to be true as well. When in shamanic states of consciousness, we understand that time is circular, linking us with our soul (and all souls) and with Infinity. There is no greater joy than this.

In a variety of spiritual traditions, the "call and response" ritual invokes the gods, goddesses, and soul guides to circle with us in the ancient circle of healing. Rituals are used in many different religions and spiritual paths as gateways or portals into the unveiling of deeper truths and sacred knowledge. The many different forms of the circle will constantly show themselves to you, and the power of its holding circle for you, often with the fire burning in its center, will continue to unveil itself. Images of the sun, the moon, the circular frame of the drum, have all been seen as they revealed their many different faces (many from behind the veil) throughout many diverse eras. This is a reminder of the power of the circle—and of the circle of life—having no beginning and no end; here the ancestors and spirit helpers hold ceremonial meetings for you and me.

When one's soul is being initiated into a higher ascension, the fire altar usually burns in the middle of the circle (in the inner vision) as the fire element reveals itself, poignantly illuminating the revelation of sacred knowledge to come. This imagery typically symbolizes a rite of passage taking place: the integration of increased soul fragments returning home to live as one within the body. This is *an initiation into the soul's ascension toward an elevated state of expanded, higher consciousness.* Here, in the circle, core truths are revealed that are usually understood to underpin and align with all nature, affirming the life/death/rebirth cycle, or "circle of incarnations," of all time. As soul seekers growing in wisdom, we recognize this unveiling as timeless, sacred truths being revealed. In the shamanic world, it is understood that the soul's fragments must be called back, invited home into the container of the body. The fire ceremony is the ceremonial ritual that signifies the transformative moment when this healing presence penetrates our inner being. We are eternally transfigured, from the inside out in this physical body, when this occurs. Once you see this in your inner vision, be sure to thank the spirits for their medicine, and circle three times to the right and three times to the left to seal the work so that no interruptive forces or destructive entities can undo the enduring power of this inner work. This sealing exercise, as daily spiritual practice, helps illuminate the importance of the psychological concept of permeable and impermeable boundaries—the difference between "that to which I allow access" and "that to which I do not allow access"—particularly when you are working in the realm of Soul.

THE CONTACT/WITHDRAWAL CYCLE (IN GESTALT TERMINOLOGY); GIVING AND RECEIVING / CONTRACTING AND EXPANDING (IN SPIRITUAL TRADITIONS)

Through this practice, the simple experience of becoming more conscious of the opening and closing inherent in all of life—also viewed as the expansion and contraction or the contact/withdrawal cycle—will be internalized as a basic principle inherent everywhere in life. We become more acutely attuned to this cycle through our breath: in the inhale breath (retrieval) and the exhale breath (release). Our breath, the beat of the drum, and our heartbeat together become the gateway to the soul's embodiment in these physical bodies. We learn that we can contain in these bodies that which we choose to contain and offer release to the rest. We begin to trust ourselves more in our ability to affirm that which we want to hold, to embody, and that which we want to surrender. We respect our instinctive choice in the matter. Our souls are always eager to remind us that we can live in a light, joyous state, not always encumbered and weighed down by the heaviness of the constant challenges of daily existence—or other people's weighty encumbrances.

Once you have tasted flight, you will forever walk the earth
with your eyes turned skyward, for there you have been,
and there you will always long to return.

LEONARDO DA VINCI

Our souls long to return skyward. Allowing yourself to go on a ride of sorts—we call this "magical flight" in shamanism—supports a phenomenological experience that is both undeniably real and specific to the soul's immediate need. You may see (through your inner vision) and feel in a visceral way (energetically) the energies of the circling of the sun and the circling of the moon, both working internally to help you retrieve inner equilibrium. You may even begin to see your circle of ancestors encircling you, with a fire altar in the center of the circle. The soul's imagery, with its song and the circle of the frame drum, will carry you away toward a landscape where you begin to see for yourself your own soul's knowledge (gnosis) unfolding. You may even begin to hear your own heartbeat or chant or rhythm. Follow your own song with its own beat and allow yourself to be carried away, perhaps by the medicine from a winged creature or a color or a specific vibration. Ride the wave, essentially, of where your own soul wants to take you. Feel free to dialogue with the beings from the Soul Realm; as you listen inside and hear words, be comfortable enough to answer back or ask for more (remembering this is the path of direct revelation). Feed the dialogue with your soul just as you would with a good friend. Sensation will be awakened and expanded as you practice staying inside your own internal imagery, using your sensation as a gateway into something more. From this place, kernels of wisdom very specific to your intention or your soul's deeper request will appear. As this new information is accessed, the "old skins" must go. This release-and-retrieval process sometimes creates a shaking or trembling in your body as you surrender to being newly configured in your soul's being. Don't be afraid. Allow it to happen. This is simply a release of old energies leaving the container of your body, combined with an internal resurgence of new, soulful vibrations and pulses. Basically, your body is recalibrating so that it can contain your soul in its newly acquired skins.

CHAPTER 6

COMING HOME TO OUR TRUE NATURE: SOUL

> *The real voyage of discovery consists not in seeking new landscapes but in having new eyes.*
>
> MARCEL PROUST

Seeing into our soul's inner world requires a nonsecular, non-fragmentary worldview—a lens open to discovering a new and different way of perceiving ourselves and our lives. While it is not my intention to feed a division between secular and nonsecular, for this discussion it is useful to view the component parts in understanding that all of life is sacred. As systems theory attests, the whole is different from the sum of its parts; nonetheless, in order to fully view the whole it may be helpful to discuss the parts. Eventually we will see into a mirror clearly, expanding into an internal, unified whole, like the yin/yang symbol. When we live in a secular world that emphasizes the external, the material, the immediate and we bring that to our meditative state, we will not be able to see with clarity into the world of the unseen universe, the world of the soul. We will feel impatient and build frustration unless we learn to suspend the lens of this physical plane while practicing openness to another lens of perception. Our true nature, our soul, inherently recognizes that these secular values are incongruent with our soul's values and wants to awaken us so that we will be informed by a larger reality.

THE ABBEY OF GETHSEMANI

Back in the late 1970s, while a student at Calvin College, I took a month-long course in Christian mysticism with the college's chaplain of thirty years, Rev. Dale Cooper. We focused on the writings of the great Christian mystic, Thomas Merton, an American Trappist monk and a visionary for peace who understood the value of nurturing the contemplative experience. Merton frequently wrote about a "metaphysic

111

ADDICTIONS: LOSS OF ATTACHMENT TO THE SOUL

In his introduction to the 1919 edition of *Women in Love*, D. H. Lawrence discusses a "period of crisis" in which "*every man who is acutely alive is acutely wrestling with his own soul*" (my italics). Lawrence goes on to say that "the people that can bring forth the new passion, the new idea, this people will endure. Those others, that fix themselves in the old idea will perish with the new life strangled unborn within them." While the discussion of addictions is quite complicated and certainly multifactorial, anyone who has ever struggled with an addiction or witnessed a loved one's battle would agree that, at its core, an addiction is indeed a wrestling with one's own soul, symptomatic of a deep disconnect with the regenerative forces of a lit internal flame. Somehow, the beast of active addiction silences the ability to listen reverently to what the soul is longing for.

In talking about addictions, it is important to discuss early childhood trauma; the two often go hand in hand. Addictions do function to keep us separated from our soul's inner voice—this is the potentiality of the strangled unborn within, that Lawrence speaks about. Addictions, and the pursuit of an addicted life, feed the delusion that a life of escapism and survival is a "good enough" human existence and, that, in fact, this is all there is. Empty fillers become the norm for daily existence, feeding the deluded notion that escapism and that sought-after high provide the best transcendence there is. Addictions feed the illusion that the River of Forgetfulness is the norm, fostering an acceptance of a dull mind and an escapist mentality. This way of being, as a daily lifestyle, is rooted in a life of little to no reflection and introspection and certainly no interest in meditation. Trying to forget an unresolved past and live an unexamined life is the mantra for the addicted person's existence. It is not uncommon to see active, concomitant addictions functioning to block the soul's expression, as a consequence of early childhood trauma. Our souls know that the material world, with its consumerist model, is vacant of sustenance meaningful enough to heal the quiet desperation that so many choose to accept as normal.

A practical example of this is the way addicted people in recovery often talk about "that little birdie on my shoulder." There is the voice of addiction talking internally, which feeds the addictive cycle, and then there is this other voice (as all addicts will attest)—the quieter voice of soul—the "other little birdie," or the winged creature trying to talk back to the addiction through positive, inner self-talk, offering another option. If responded to, this inner, quiet voice will call forth an awakening into greater health and wellness. Renewed attachment with soul will result, automatically nurturing a developing personal power and strength of will. Learning to listen—to wake up—to this still, small voice is what will connect each of us with our soul's priorities and the basic principles of the Soul Realm. Qualities such as truth, purity, light, love, and beauty are the ingredients found in our elemental nature, our soul, and, if we allow them, they will be a powerful force of will that overpowers the delusion of addiction.

People who struggle severely with addictions often have an early childhood history of trauma, most of which is often blocked off from conscious awareness, remaining unprocessed. The one gift, if we could call it that, of trauma for many is early awakening, attachment, and deep belief in the Spirit World—the Soul Realm—as the bodymind's adaptive response to trauma. Instinctively, the soul knows how to reframe something traumatic into something transcendent and redemptive. According to shamanic methodology, chronic pain and suffering actually feed an out-of-body experience for the soul, which propels the soul to travel back to its native land, the Soul Realm. In fact, those who have lived a life of trauma often experience a "privileged access" in communication with wise beings because this was their primary means of survival. The psychological term for this is "disassociation" or "depersonalization." These trauma survivors have a unique skill set for traversing the Soul Realm, because it is familiar to them. Usually, their creative adaptation to the trauma has been to "fly away" into a transcendent state. Trauma is in fact another gateway or bridge into the transcendent experience, once we work through the trauma to see to the other side. These are the gifts gained through the pain of both trauma and addictions. This privileged access, developed over years of creative adaptations, can be utilized as a bridge to launch more deeply into an appreciation of the Soul Realm to aid in daily living—once fully appreciated.

We humans seek many different paths as a gateway to soul attachment or as an avoidant expression of running away from soul. Often we spend many lengthy years of our lives trying to discount our soul's calling. Jungian analyst James Hillman echoes this theme when he states, "Psychology regards all symptoms to be expressing the right thing in the wrong way." A preoccupation with pornography or romance novels, for example, may come as a presenting symptom dominating a passionate person whose disowned quest for love has degenerated into an obsession or preoccupation with images of sex and love. "Follow the lead of your symptoms," Hillman suggests, "for there's usually a myth in the mess, and a mess is an expression of soul."

The modern astrophysicist Dr. Neil deGrasse Tyson talks about our human connection and belonging with the basic, key ingredients of the universe. In order of quantity, the universe and our bodies are made up of the same primary components. Our bodies are made up primarily of water (the sacral chakra is the water element), water being made up of two parts hydrogen and one part oxygen, leaving us made up primarily of hydrogen and oxygen. The cosmos's two most highly abundant elements are hydrogen and oxygen, as well. It is indisputable that our biology is linked to the richness and the chemistry of the cosmos. Spiritual, mystical traditions have known that we match the universe and are joined with it, even before science confirmed this. Now, science is discovering and confirming what we have known intrinsically for ages: that we are, indeed, all connected, as we can see in a very finite way in the elements of the periodic table. As we come home to these basic, elemental truths of the universe, the connection between the earth, water, fire, air, and ether elements in our own bodies becomes clearer. This balance will invite the soul to live in peace in this physical realm and will allow us to engage more completely with the world around us.

CHAPTER 7
SHEDDING THE OLD SKINS: LEARNING TO UNLEARN TO RELEARN

> *Consciously or unconsciously, the mind is always seeking something. . . .*
> *It is only when the mind is completely still that there can be a*
> *possibility of touching the deeper waters.*
>
> J. KRISHNAMURTI[1]

As we respect the revelation of information from Soul, we then can more clearly see our true nature, our soul. We understand the difference between the limitations of our wounded selves and the infinite, majestic powers that lie inherent in our soul. In this clarity of distinction, we begin to perceive our ancestral connections more clearly. We see the way in which our soul is circled by the spiritual beings who exist to protect its evolutionary development and unfolding. Many clients have talked about seeing their bones and perhaps feeling as if they experienced themselves as a primordial rock, emanating with colors, power, and healing vibrational qualities.

CASE STUDY: TERESA HEARS HER SOUL'S VOICE

A teenage client suffering from anorexia, whom I'll call Teresa, connected with an image of the sea meeting a shore of rocks instead of sand. As she processed the "familiar ditch" in which she found herself, she confronted her "recovery self" versus her "eating-disordered self" and the belief that she had to choose which self she was going to allow to guide her in her movement forward. Throughout her session, the healing energies of both the water element and rock, the earth element, helped Teresa to see both her solidity of strength and her need for adaptability and acceptance of movement. The knowledge from her soul emanated throughout her inner vision, revealing conscious information that allowed her to choose change in order to heal in her recovery. Even at fifteen years of age, Teresa clearly heard her soul's voice, versus the parasitic quality of her eating-disordered voice that was eating away at her inner, true nature. As in Teresa's case, once we learn to recognize and value the information when it comes through, we begin to see how it makes sense, as we allow its wisdom to unfold. The puzzle pieces come together and we begin to see the full picture.

TRUST THE UNVEILING

> *Tradition means giving votes to the most obscure of all classes, our ancestors. It is the democracy of the dead.*
>
> G. K. CHESTERTON

As the veil is lifted, we begin to see clearly our soul's true nature, which is deeply connected to nature, our ancestors, and the elements. Earth, water, fire, air, and ether will function as medicinal aids, teaching us deep and lasting truths about rooting in the earth; being carried by the River of Life; yielding to the fire to find transformation; and ultimately, lifting up, consumed by air, thereby merging into deep union with transcendence. We learn to trust the flow of life, especially in times of the unknown, just as we remember that spring consistently follows winter and the sun does rise every morning. The "all-oneness," as opposed to the aloneness, becomes a trustworthy experience as we allow ourselves to be comforted by the omniscient presence of nature and our ancestors. Even though our life circumstances may have us feeling alone and fearful in a dark night of the soul, our souls will awaken us to more of an inner seer sight, a reality of internal support and connection with all beings, as we find trust and comfort in the Soul Realm.

Many clients, as a result of initiation through fire ceremonies, describe themselves as being awakened to a new self, a being filled with brighter light, expanded love, a greater appreciation for simple beauty, and an enriched connection to their core truth. This is the frequency of knowing in which our soul vibrates, regardless of the circumstances of our lives. Again, our soul does not see us as a being of woundedness but as a constant being of power, love, and light. This constancy of ever-present sourcing awaits our communion, if only we would allow ourselves to remain plugged in. Kokopelli, a fertility deity often present in a fire ceremony, can be imaged in the inner vision, holding the space for this transformation to occur.

The fire ceremony as initiation is the significant ritual that confirms new beginnings, new patterns, and new behaviors. In ancient Egypt, the ceremony of lighting the fire was celebrated annually as the people created a festival of light with candles, lanterns, and lamps. It was believed that this stimulated the flame's awakening, representing the light journey back to the ancestors and gods and goddesses. Many cultures throughout time have circled around the dancing flame to awaken powerful energies and confirm initiates to their position in the tribe. When you see the

KOKOPELLI

fire ceremony in the inner visions of your meditations, know that it is a confirmation for you of a renewed ownership of sacred knowledge and a more integrated skill set of soul's consciousness. Through the burning away of the old, the new dance emerges. Often we can experience more lightness of being after receiving the medicine of the fire ceremony. Kokopelli may appear, to play his flute and help support us in our resurrected dance. Many clients have seen the ancestors holding the circle for them while they dance or sit in the center of the fire circle, receiving new wisdom. Notice which ancestors sit with you, and revere their visitations. Look to see their faces and hear their words. Bow in gratitude once you feel completely seen in their presence. Let all the beings know that you see them and that you will be back to visit them more often. Feel the energies of their ancestral medicine that is being imparted to you so that you can bring it into the actions of your present life.

Often in shamanic meditation, when the fire altar emerges, we are reminded of the circle that is always circling for us and the fire that is constantly burning for each one of us, as our ancestors and spirit guides hold constant circle. When we see the circle with the fire in the center (in our inner vision), this is the reminder that *sacred holy space* is being held for each one of us to expand into greater spaciousness of consciousness; to circle with our ancestors, our spirit helpers, our soul guides, and the beings who long for our healing and emergence is to enter into the metaphorical "Holy of Holies." When our soul's inner flame is lit in our internal temple, sacred mysteries are unveiled through direct revelation. Their sole purpose in the Soul Realm is to support our emergence into new, expansive, and unlimited fullness of our soul's potentiality. This means that we must always be shedding old behaviors that no longer function constructively for us. To live a daily lifestyle of release and retrieval means to let go of the human emotion that fosters constriction, living small, and instead to open to our soul's expansiveness of being. To remind ourselves of this soul reality, we practice daily—both individually and within community—to remain connected to the sacred truths from this otherworldly sphere.

SHEDDING THE OLD SKINS, RETRIEVING NEW SKINS.
EXPANDING INTO NEW COGNITION, NEW AFFECT,
NEW BEHAVIORS.

The Release and Retrieval Process

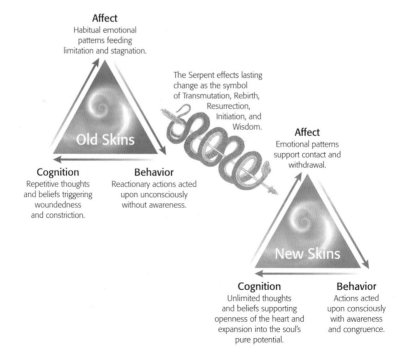

Affect
Habitual emotional patterns feeding limitation and stagnation.

The Serpent effects lasting change as the symbol of Transmutation, Rebirth, Resurrection, Initiation, and Wisdom.

Old Skins

Cognition
Repetitive thoughts and beliefs triggering woundedness and constriction.

Behavior
Reactionary actions acted upon unconsciously without awareness.

Affect
Emotional patterns support contact and withdrawal.

New Skins

Cognition
Unlimited thoughts and beliefs supporting openness of the heart and expansion into the soul's pure potential.

Behavior
Actions acted upon consciously with awareness and congruence.

Control of the mind is the most challenging and the most rewarding of human tasks, and the Buddha does not underestimate its difficulties. The mind, he suggests, has a depth far greater than the deepest sea, and all the way down it churns with emotional tempests of which we are barely conscious, but which virtually dictate thought and behavior.

EKNATH EASWARAN

When we are greeted by our soul guides or animal teachers, we enter into dialogue with them. Soul helpers, spirit guides, power animals, and all beings who enter into our sacred intention of expanding consciousness exist only to help us and to respond directly to our pursuit for knowledge. Ask your questions directly to them. Be brave. Repeat these questions if the response is not understood the first time, or the second, or the third. Clarify directly by asking, *"Are you my teacher?"* State your intention and continue to restate until you have the understanding and clarity you need. As Jesus taught us, "Ask, and it shall be given to you; seek, and you shall find; knock, and it shall be opened to you" (Matthew 7:7). Or, as the prophet Jeremiah said in the Bible, "Thus says the Lord, 'Stand by the ways and see and ask for the ancient paths, Where the good way is, and walk in it; And you shall find rest for your souls.' But they said, 'We will not walk in it. And I set watchmen over you, saying, Listen to the sound of the trumpet.' But they said, 'We will not listen'" (Jeremiah 6:16).

Asking according to the ancient shamanic path and setting a simple but specific intention might sound something like this:

I call upon the Soul-Realm, asking all my soul guides and animal helpers to guide me deeper into light, clarity, truth, and love. Thy will be done, and please, align me with thy will as I ask that . . . (speaking your intention clearly)

Perhaps you are interested in releasing an old habitual behavioral pattern and you need help with this. *Just ask.* Whatever it is that you seek, know that your soul and the Soul Realm are eager to help you—while remembering of course that this does not mean that we *always* get what we ask for. As we grow in spiritual maturity, harnessing an unshakeable

usually a symbolic representation of the *unknown* and an invitation to enter into "the dark," the fertile void not yet revealed—always an initiation into a higher, more enlightened realm.

Whatever occurs, the result will be a developed sight into the unseen universe. Sight or knowing may come without words, perhaps through an experience of comfort and/or peaceful sensations (not necessarily seeing an image with a clear picture). Sometimes a graphic image that is not so peaceful may also reveal itself (the Soul Realm is not always compassionate in its truth telling), because dismemberment must occur before re-membering. Whatever comes in the inner vision, keep trusting it, staying with it, asking, "Are you my soul's teacher?" And, "What is it that you want me to understand?" The process of learning to practice presence to all that comes will lead to an experience of deepened trust in the unknown, hidden realms.

THE CRONE WOMAN AND SAGES AS KEEPERS OF THE WISE MYSTERIES

Honoring the role of the divine feminine in healing ourselves and healing the planet is essential. Patriarchy and religious emphases on God as male has wreaked havoc on our souls (which seek balance) as well as the balance of the planet. It is through honoring the path of the feminine and the women healers (as well as the masculine and the male healers) who show up to heal us in the Soul Realm that we will find greater harmony on earth, beginning with greater harmony within. The great white light, with its moon consciousness, along with Crone Woman, often beckons us to keep going deeper, into *seeing* more of the sacred mysteries in the unseen universe. These moments of enlightened consciousness are the honey of the transformational encounter, when sacred masculine and sacred feminine become more intimately entwined in greater unity in our inner bodies. Here, in these magical moments, the memories of the ancient soul will be revealed—the seed of memory that Plato discusses continues to blossom and unfold, offering useful information that makes sense inside.

In the Soul Realm, there is no separation of past and future, so the present moment will be pregnant with the fluidity of time and timelessness. Each moment will be fertile with the knowing and the understanding of the soul's many different incarnations *if* we remain receptive to seeing. Do not be afraid to go here . . . your soul is hoping you will be brave. The information retrieved will only assist in providing greater understanding of your soul's purpose and how you fit into the larger Whole.

THE PENETRATING EYES

I cannot pretend to describe in full detail the mystical experiences that await you, but I can say that, often, penetrating eyes will appear to awaken and stimulate your third eye or your pineal gland, so that your inner vision will be awakened more crisply (often reminiscent of a peacock's feathers). Remember that this is a path of direct revelation, each visitation designed to assist you in seeing more clearly into the Soul Realm. Your inner eye will recognize the piercing eyes of the ascended beings from the upper world or the gazing eyes from the visitations of particular animal spirits. These may be the penetrating eyes of your power animal or of Jesus or even a powerful ascended mystical being living in the Soul Realm, wanting to offer you healing. If you initially feel afraid to look, do not hesitate to maintain contact; keep looking to see more and to ask more. In this place of face-to-face encounter with the Soul Realm, you will know that you are known and you will know that you are seen. There is *no more hiding*.

The old shame from past wounding experiences, which kept you hiding and living small, will begin to fall away. Like the snake shedding its skin, you will feel the release of old, painful memories or the cleansing of traumatic imprints. You will experience more infinite space within as the medicine from these penetrating eyes reveals pure healing intention and functions to stimulate your third eye, opening and attuning internal energies to a higher frequency. You will feel as though you are being lifted with an internal explosion of good feeling, peace, and calm. Problem solving often results from this place as the wisdom mind opens and the duality and constriction of the busy brain melt away. As thousands of clients have reported, the medicine from the Soul Realm can actually shift the brain's frequency. Remember, the brain is an electrochemical instrument that organically responds to soul's vibrational healing energies. When you experience this firsthand, you will understand what I am writing about.

When dialoguing with your soul and the Soul Realm, remain open to receive that which is trying to show itself to you. When a creature appears, invite it in—again, provided you have circled with your spirit protectors and asked, "Are you my helper?" Notice your own degree of receptivity; if you are hesitant and skeptical and closing off or shutting down, the Soul Realm will be less available to you. Remember, we are trying to remember what the River of Forgetfulness wants us to forget. We are simply allowing the veil to be lifted. There is very little we must do here other than quiet our busy brains and allow the information to flow *in*. We are simply *reclaiming* in present-day awareness a new self-perception as divine personality, as soul. In this expanded state of consciousness, the formless takes form; the invisible becomes visible; the unseen, seen.

Whether you believe the information is coming from the collective unconscious, your imagination, your own intuition, or your soul, it is important to acknowledge the divine presence, with its wisdom amidst all the mystery. Calling in the energies that awaken embodied enlightenment is what opens us to more balance and greater wisdom and compassion, fostering an inner peace and a surprising repeated return to unconditional love. Remember that the soul is interested in helping you flow on a specific frequency. The woundedness, with its constricting imprint, wants to shut down that flow (tight fist versus open palm). It is the medicine that comes in from the Soul Realm that is specific to what you need and will elevate you to a higher frequency of your own soul's expression.

CHAPTER 8:

BECOMING MORE "ME": MY TRUE NATURE EMBODIED

In both mythology and literature there are different depictions and associations with the soul. D. H. Lawrence wrote a poem entitled "Terra Incognita" that is, from a literary perspective, quite consistent with the material of this book. It reads like this:

There are vast realms of consciousness still undreamed of
vast ranges of experience, like the humming of unseen harps,
we know nothing of, within us.

Oh when man has escaped from the barbed-wire entanglement
of his own ideas and his own mechanical devices
there is a marvelous rich world of contact and sheer fluid beauty
and fearless face-to-face awareness of now-naked life
and me, and you, and other men and women
and grapes, and ghouls, and ghosts and green moonlight
and ruddy-orange limbs stirring the limbo
of the unknown air, and eyes so soft
softer than the space between the stars.
And all things, and nothing, and being and not-being
alternately palpitate,
when at last we escape the barbed-wire enclosure
of Know-Thyself, knowing we can never know,
we can but touch, and wonder, and ponder, and make our effort
and dangle in a last fastidious fine delight
as the fuchsia does, dangling her reckless drop
of purple after so much putting forth
and slow mounting marvel of a little tree.

Learning to stay open to the messages from the Soul Realm is what nature and Holy Mystery invite us to do as a daily practice of living life, traversing the two worlds of matter and spirit. This openness is not suggested as another thing "I must do" but as a way of being present to every moment of every day—as a daily exercise in living each moment of your life as devotional spiritual practice.

Our bodies are supported by earth's elemental energies, whether we acknowledge this fact or not. We, unfortunately, are not always aware of how much effort we exude in holding ourselves up, or perhaps how much strain we put on our neck, throat, and jaw in order to support our head. Just take a moment to notice how you are holding yourself in your body. Where in your body are you exhibiting tension? Feel the way your throat and your shoulders are holding up your head, as opposed to a little relaxing of your shoulders in the direction of your hips. Allow for more space in the throat, which will enable the connection between your head and your heart to allow greater fluidity and ease of connectivity. Experience your head feeling free to move, even lifting up without pressure, as if opening to the expansiveness of the bright blue sky. Often, when we try to create internal space, the body responds with tightness around the neck and effort, held in the ears and the jaw, to keep everything contained. Some clients even experience the stress and tension in the teeth and the jaw, from years of withholding free speech and expression. I have actually observed many clients' mouths get tight and reduce in size as mouths lock and jaws implode with information that is struggling to emerge to the surface, where it would find release and relief. The coming up and out through the process of honoring movement is simply learning to no longer implode. Instead, allow your own natural flow to be rhythmically reclaimed and the internal flame to be rekindled. Learning to release what must go and retrieve the new information that wants to flow in is a daily spiritual practice when you are living attached to your own soul.

See if you can move your breath into whatever parts of your body are locking in tension right now. Allow yourself to lie on the floor and experience the different sensations of being held and supported by the ground of earth. It's a good experiment to begin to become more conscious of the earth as our foundation, our stability, our constant, sure, reliable, and steady *support*. Know, in the same way that you are learning to trust that the earth is supporting and holding you, that you can begin to apply the same truth to your soul. Try to feed a new belief within, affirming through inner self-dialogue, "*I can trust my soul as my primary internal support for daily living.*"

OUR ANCIENT MEMORY OF BEING HELD

The experience of being held is ancient, reminiscent of being held in the womb, the primordial waters. As we learn to trust that the River of Life can truly carry us each and every day, we will affirm the reminder that life's circumstances can be trusted. Even as startling and disturbing challenges unfold, we can remind ourselves of the memory of being carried and cared for in the Soul Realm. Perhaps we can imagine our fears, worries, and anxieties like an ocean wave rolling back out to sea to be met by the vastness of the ocean's expanse. With a new internal space (from the release of tension, anxiety, and worry), we can awaken to create greater spaciousness: to breathe, to trust, to settle inward, allowing ourselves to nourish greater internal union, feeling a connection and oneness with the realm of Soul. This is the experience that many yogis have when in savasana, surrender-to-death pose, on the yoga mat. As so many yoga teachers have reminded me, the challenge is to bring our yoga "off the mat." This is the challenge of being human spirits. Moment to moment, we are learning to bring the transcendent soul's reality to the physical human experience. Life lived from a soulful perspective will then unfold into the soul's destiny and be fulfilled one day at a time.

As you perceive yourself as "Soul Retrieved as Beloved," you will awaken to some of the more powerful beings in the Soul Realm—those eager to appear, to do your healing work, transforming you from dismemberment to re-membering and transmutation, effecting the shedding of the old skins to be replaced by new. Remembering that so many of the more powerful beings in the Soul Realm share their names with primary yoga poses—crow, cobra, tree, and half-moon poses and sun salutations—perhaps explore working with one of these poses at home each week while inviting the medicine of its being to share its healing power with you. While I will emphasize that the philosophy underpinning yoga is quite thorough and profound, it is fascinating to me that the yoga philosophies have multiple similarities with shamanic methodology and Gestalt therapy and theory, as embodied mysticisms rooted in phenomenology. I learned recently that full- and new-moon days are observed by purists as yoga holidays in the ashtanga yoga tradition. While working with the cycles of the moon, you will discover that these are days when the veil is thin and our ethereal awareness is potentially heightened. If you allow yourself to stay open to incorporating the organic rhythms of nature and allow this practice to function daily as experiment, you will find yourself designing and implementing your own personal spiritual practice. You will, undoubtedly, experience a deepened inner vision as you dialogue with the Soul Realm on these powerful days. As you continue to grow your roots into your own embodied soul—deepening into the earth element—allow your attachment, like the umbilical cord, to connect you belly to belly with Holy Mystery.

Practice your connection with your elemental self-balancing energies of earth, water, fire, air, and ether through elemental breath work. See essential characteristics of your soul's true nature being reflected back through nature as you observe and commune daily with the elements. Shamanism teaches us to allow the rocks and trees and all life to give voice to the dialogue with our soul. Notice yourself being "listened into speech" as the elements offer you comfort, clarity, calming, or deepened understanding. As we come home to our true natures, our souls, we will begin to experience a kindred spirit with these elements, and their various characteristics will resonate inside us. We human beings are about 70 percent water. Just like the tides of the sea, we are affected by the phases of the moon. Tides are created because the earth and the moon are attracted to each other, like magnets. The moon, in its moon consciousness, tries to pull anything on the earth to bring it closer, including our souls. At night, try the experiment of conscious and deliberate breath, inhaling and exhaling in relationship to the moon; feel the energy of the moon's awareness of contraction and expansion as you resonate in your breath with the pulse of all life. Just as the phases of the moon are determined by its relative position to the sun, so too will our spiritual practice be affected by the ebbs and flows of nature. Full moons occur when the sun and moon are in opposition, and new moons, when they are in conjunction. So too will we have our days when we feel more connected with our souls than on other days. Remember that, just as both sun and moon exert a gravitational pull on the earth, so too does the Soul Realm exert a gravitational pull on our souls, giving us the opportunity to practice listening and responding to this hidden reality.

As the *Farmers' Almanac* recommends planting seeds at the new moon, when the rooting force is strongest, and transplanting at the full moon, when the flowering force is strongest, we too can learn to work with natural cycles in relationship to our "soil," our soul and the manifestation of our soul's destiny. Dialoguing with the Soul Realm over time makes us more attuned to natural cycles' ebb and flow. Observing moon days is one way to grow in the recognition of the rhythms of nature so that we can live in greater harmony with the Soul Realm and with the earth.[1]

BODY SPLITS AND POLARITIES UNIFIED

Do you not know that you are the temple of God, and that the Spirit of God dwells in you?

CORINTHIANS 3:16

As human spirits, we are either imprisoned in conflictual opposition or liberated into mysterious paradox. Through these bodily temples that house our human existence, we learn how to merge and unify and integrate both our humanity and our divinity. This human body invites as our essential task the revelation of hidden unity as we allow all sides of an issue, or pairs of opposites, to exist in equal dignity and worth—similarly to the way in which the yin/yang symbol holds the Whole.

As we learn to embrace all of this (the yin and the yang, the darkness and the light, the human and the spiritual) in the container of our bodies, we realize that life's circumstances offer us initiation into an embodiment of wisdom gained through the life lessons of our soul's evolutionary growth toward enlightenment. The enlightened state is nothing more than a conscious, deepened embodiment of our divinity in this physical body. It is in these bodies that we meet God in every moment, as we breathe into each breath with a full presence. The soul is our teacher, our holy guide, empowering us through the lesson of unconditional love—first, self-love, which comes through a true understanding of the compassionate love from the Beloved, so beautifully expressed in the sacred text of the Song of Solomon, "I am my Beloved's and my Beloved is Mine" (Song of Solomon 6:13).

From this richness, we are then able to offer love to others. As we learn to balance the energies of earth, water, fire, air, and ether in our bodies, these human containers can begin to function as fluidly as water and as adaptably as air, able to contract and expand with the movement of life, including the upsets, the seemingly undesirable trials and unasked-for tribulations. Ideally, we become more aware of our moment-to-moment decisions to exercise our free will to choose, or not choose, either constructive or destructive thoughts; whether to gestate, and for how long, the positive or negative emotions; and we learn which actions to consciously foster, the reactive behaviors guided by the wounded personality or the wiser, higher-mind actions edified by the Soul Realm. Herein lies the opportunity to begin to feel more *positively in control* of our lives and live from a connection and an alignment with our true nature, our divinity. This connection, the more we feed it, will feed us; there is reciprocity here. We will no longer have an experience of fleeting communion with our soul (or of complete detachment from it) but instead will feel a deep attachment that cannot be broken. Again, this attachment grows in the daily experience as experiment: "*Which do I feed?*" is the ongoing, inner self-dialogue. That which we feed will produce the result, or the fruits, of the soul. This work is known as "the cultivation of the heart," the path of unconditional love, which is the vibration of the soul. Even if we find ourselves being initially reactive in the relationships of our lives, our soul will remind us to try again and open, yet again, to the path of unconditional love. Owning our humanness (with all its wounding and its proneness to being reactive) is essential to the process of opening up to a responsible response, i.e., one rooted not in reactivity but in compassion, love, and wisdom. Our soul instinctively knows how to do this if we allow ourselves to listen to that innermost voice.

Two Recommended Exercises to Increase Awareness of Body Splits and Engage in Unification:

1. Sit comfortably, holding both hands in front, and feel the four fingers and thumb of one hand touch the four fingers and thumb of the other hand. Breathe your breath into the union of your two hands, each finger point connecting to the other, feeding fluid energy back and forth between the two. Experience your internal body, like a white column, filling with internal union, the two becoming one. This experience of the two hands merging into one is similar to the way in which we desire that the internal body meld together where the splits occur. Visualize white light (like the full-moon luminescence) or golden/red/orange light (like the radiant sun) energetically sealing the two parts of the split as one unified whole—as though zipping up the healing energies of sun and moon consciousness. Work with what appears; sometimes it is more sun energy, because that is what is needed, and sometimes it is more moon energy. Opening to both sun and moon energies in balance is what matters.

2. Lie on the earth in a comfortable position. Bend your knees and bring your feet together, flat on floor, with their soles touching each other—this is called Goddess pose in yoga. Experience your spine relaxing into the floor and feel your upper arms resting, even sinking, into the earth. Support your body in melting into the ground of your being, earth energies, experiencing the merging, the unifying. Bring your hands and fingers together again, touching, as in exercise 1, as they rest gently around your heart / solar plexus area. Imagine the finger points merging into one entity. Experience this medicinal force in your body again and notice the body splits healing, as if by a force searing the split into a healed whole. Breathe your breath into the tight spaces and imagine white light or golden-red light, like a needle and thread, unifying the inner body. Be grateful. Let this healing medicine know you now have eyes to see and ears to hear and that you understand what is being offered as medicine to aid in

your healing. This acknowledgement is essential, enabling greater healing powers to flow your way. Doubt and skepticism interrupt the flow of the ancient healing waters.

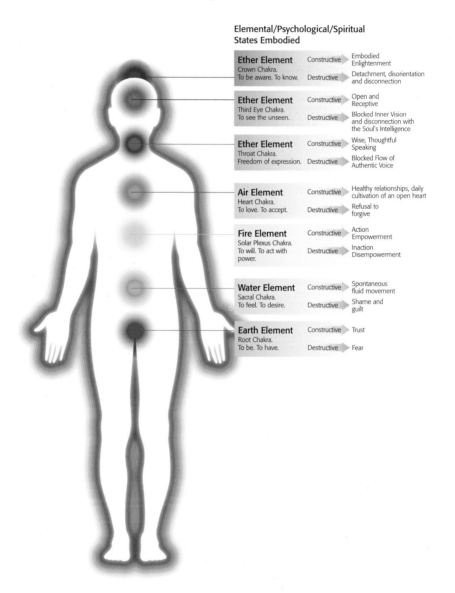

Elemental/Psychological/Spiritual
States Embodied

Ether Element   Constructive   Embodied Enlightenment
Crown Chakra.
To be aware. To know.   Destructive   Detachment, disorientation and disconnection

Ether Element   Constructive   Open and Receptive
Third Eye Chakra.
To see the unseen.   Destructive   Blocked Inner Vision and disconnection with the Soul's Intelligence

Ether Element   Constructive   Wise, Thoughtful Speaking
Throat Chakra.
Freedom of expression.   Destructive   Blocked Flow of Authentic Voice

Air Element   Constructive   Healthy relationships, daily cultivation of an open heart
Heart Chakra.
To love. To accept.   Destructive   Refusal to forgive

Fire Element   Constructive   Action Empowerment
Solar Plexus Chakra.
To will. To act with power.   Destructive   Inaction Disempowerment

Water Element   Constructive   Spontaneous fluid movement
Sacral Chakra.
To feel. To desire.   Destructive   Shame and guilt

Earth Element   Constructive   Trust
Root Chakra.
To be. To have.   Destructive   Fear

BEING REFLECTIVE (SOUL'S DESIRE) VS.
REACTIVE (HUMAN WOUNDING)

As the busy brain continues to quiet into embracing acceptance and stillness, we move into the flow, or the dance, of the contraction and expansion of the breath of life, and we experience ourselves as interconnected with all living beings through the pulsation of sacred life. By attending to our breath, we learn to honor our movement toward and away from all life. The Gestalt theory of awareness cycle also acknowledges the movement toward contact and the movement toward withdrawal as we learn to allow ourselves to self-regulate.

When we experience ourselves in an expansive state, we are open to the retrieval of a renewed spaciousness. Honoring our organic self-regulation, our movement toward contact and withdrawal, will allow us to internalize the experience, making it our own in a personal, individual, and meaningful way. Opening and opening again to our soul's phenomenology allows Sacred Mystery to provide confirmation that sacred information is available for us and can indeed be accessed and trusted, moment to moment, for our soul's expression.

When we find ourselves being reactive in the relationships of our lives, it is often a symptom of a lack of a unified internal structure. When we have internal body splits (duality within), with aspects of ourselves cut off from other aspects, these fractured parts create internal conflict and feed the disharmony within, which will be acted out on the external environment. Learning to be a safe container for the soul to come home to means that we want to become more self-aware of the ways in which we act out on the outside world. In other words, our internal environment can become our external environmental field. This discerning understanding can become the motivator for healing and attending to the woundedness of the inner world, offering unification of being: mind, body, and soul unified as one, like an aligned arrow with soft, flexible feathers. Through this awareness, we first experience congruence in the internal world and then the external world begins to manifest that which we already are on the inside. This is simply alignment of purpose, congruency of inner and outer worlds, joined as one. Once we are aligned, congruent, and spacious on the inside, we are then capable of entering into magical flights through shamanic and meditative journeys as well.

This is where we see opportunities to access magical powers and manifest our soul's destiny in this physical plane. The two worlds meet and are constantly informing each other—the physical and the spiritual—in these bodies as we allow our souls to guide our actions in daily living.

LIVING WITH MOMENT-TO-MOMENT AWARENESS

Try to commit to the daily practice of ethereal presence (initially ten to fifteen minutes each day) in both your inner world of imagery and vision and the outer world of nature, the larger environmental field. Stay open to the surprise conversations each day that allow you to breathe and stretch into an expanded reality, to inform your understanding of the Soul Realm. For example, recently I went to the drive-thru at the bank, thinking that I would make a quick deposit. Much to my surprise, the bank teller started talking with me about an experience she had at 7 a.m. that morning. As she explained it, she was driving to work when the mist on the water of Lake Carnegie called to her so profoundly that she said she had to pull over on the side of the road to sit. Instinctively, she knew she needed to be present to the water and "listen to the lake," and she responded to this nudging. She explained in great detail the words of comfort she heard in her interior world and the way in which these words were so perfectly crafted that it seemed as if "someone had to know just what I was going through." I explained that this was a totemic or shamanic experience wherein nature called to her to speak directly to the depths of her soul in her specific life experience.

The Lady of the Lake, in Celtic shamanism, is the one who "lifts the veil," so that we might see more clearly and not be clouded by the mist. The mist is the image used in many different spiritual traditions to represent the way in which the veil can be lifted for us, or we can be awakened by the Soul Realm to understand more fully the otherworldly realm. The key is that we must all learn how to respond to this inner calling. This bank teller agreed that this experience for her was in fact a totemic experience. We can all have daily experiences like this one as we learn to practice receptivity to the natural world, which is alive all around us and eager to engage.

As you allow yourself to have more of these spontaneous experiences with the Soul Realm (and with other humans), visualize yourself being reconfigured in the true expression of your soul. As my client who in psychotherapy was working with this material for months exclaimed, "I am becoming someone who reminds me of myself." This was her recognition of her soul coming home into greater consciousness in an integrated, practical, and embodied way. Allow yourself to utilize nature as your playground, dialoguing freely with the different beings who show up to offer you their medicine.

When I was receiving a massage from a colleague who integrates shamanism into her massage practice, I had an amazing, spontaneous "aha" moment. I was specific in my need to address an old wound in my body, remnants of fear, helplessness, and panic residing in my core trunk. As I was imagining my life's circumstances, wherein I was standing up, alone, to a local bank, old core themes were coming afloat like sludge. I was refusing to allow my house to be collateral for a business loan, and this action was triggering old wounds of "standing up to authoritative powers." While I was lying on the table, I called in my power animals. Who showed up? First of all were the darling leprechauns, providing their magic dust on the conference tables at the bank. Second arrived Pegasus, my white horse with wings, who has lived as my power animal on the right side of my body—the masculine side—since I was a girl. I internally welcomed Pegasus, and then suddenly, the massage therapist exclaimed, "Oh, my God! I see this white horse with huge wings." *I had not said a single word to her about my power animal's presence.* We both burst into tears as we shared the recognition of the power of the ethereal world. We celebrated this shared moment, wherein we both "had eyes to see" together. This, for us, was such a welcomed source of affirmation. There is so much doubt and skepticism that is often offered in regard to this work that moments like this are deeply treasured. Needless to say, my jaguar (who lives on the left side of my body) then entered as my power animal protecting my feminine side. And then White Owl spread its wings across my body and pierced my face with its gaze, reminding me that I was protected in this unfolding of "woman against bank."

The next day, as I drummed further about this issue, I saw a feminine hand holding a brightly shining egg. An egg! The symbol of rebirth and resurrection. Thus shored up, I found the courage and strength and personal power to talk back to the layers of fear and constriction. As I practiced waiting for the unknown to unfold, I supported myself with these internal visions. Weeks later, I heard from the bank. My house was removed as collateral on the business loan—which both my accountants and lawyers agreed was a miracle they hadn't believed would happen.

Each of us has many stories to tell about the challenges of life and the miracles that surprise us and remind us to trust in the wondrous magic that is available for us through this magico-mystical practice. Gestalt theory's practice of "internal supports" helps us reinforce an inner self-dialogue and learn to talk back to life's potentially intimidating circumstances when they arise. It is always more productive when we approach the situations of our lives with an inner clarity, receptivity rather than reactivity, and a more heightened awareness. The daily practice of "incarnation"—soul embodiment—will help with this. We begin to understand more clearly that we can either react to the circumstances of our lives from a place of our limited, wounded personality (which consistently fosters reactivity) or choose to trust and open ourselves to being our best and responding with our best, most loving and life-affirming response (which is what our soul knows how to do).

By the time you finish reading this book, you will experience and start to understand the imagery and language of your soul. You will begin to notice yourself moving through the world in new ways, with new eyes. You will feel more connected from the inside, with knowledge of who you are in the eyes of the Beloved. Once you understand how beloved you are in the eyes of your soul, then you will begin to understand that your core essence, and all that matters, is *love*. You are *loved* and *you are love*. However corny this sounds, trust me, this information is affirmed daily as I work with my clients, and I have witnessed hundreds of clients who are amazed by the power of this work. You will begin to feel an energy bursting from inside your chest, transferring vibrations out into the world from your heart space and your third eye. You will experience transcendent sensations of ecstasy, bliss, love, light, beauty, and truth, which are the awakened vibrations (or humming) of soul activity. These are the only vibrations your soul wants to experience.

The more you experience this deep, unconditional love, the more you'll want to abide here as well. These states are natural and organic to your soul's true vibration. As you learn to feed this love internally, you will naturally want to share it with the larger world. As the Rev. Dr. Carter Heyward eloquently states:

> Love is a choice—not simply, or necessarily, a rational choice, but rather a willingness to be present to others without pretense or guide. Love is a conversion to humanity—a willingness to participate with others in the healing of a broken world and broken lives. Love is the choice to experience life as a member of the human family, a partner in the dance of life.

As you read these words, they should resonate with your soul. As Plato wrote, "A man is just when he has a well ordered soul because then he will do the right thing by performing good and just actions." Throughout the ages, whether with the Beatles singing about love or the philosophers and poets writing about love or the theologians affirming that God is Love, this really has always been the simple, core truth of where our soul resides—in Love. As we trust daily life as the playground for deepening in our soul's ascension, we will notice that we are given lessons in mastering love.

Remember, it is the constricting vibration of the wounded personality with all its limitations that is foreign to the soul. Allow your soul's energies to lift you up to new heights. Experience a new pulsing of aliveness from within and feel the kundalini as a vital internal force supporting your spine's fullness and your courage in living the life your soul wants to be living. You will experience your erect yet flexible spine supporting your open heart as you move through the world as a whole being. Regardless of the circumstances of our lives, this transcendent sphere of Soul is the world of harmony and union with Great Mystery. Mystery carries the powers of Creation, which is constantly re-creating. As we each learn to interpret the sacred knowledge and nourish this vitality of our inner world, the world will be filled with more of us who are like-minded. Our enlightened inner worlds will have more power externally as we join together as an integrated, global community with purposeful intention, creating soulful societies.

THE SPIRIT WHO IS HOLY CREATES WHOLENESS

The Biblical prophet Isaiah exclaims, "I am about to do a new thing. Now it springs forth. Do you not perceive it?"
(ISAIAH: 43:19)

The healing beings of the Soul Realm suggest that we simply open our perception of reality as we understand it, considering that there are varying states of consciousness into which we can expand, if we allow ourselves to do so. Perceiving beyond the paradigms of past beliefs to which you may have attached yourself opens you to the possibility of a new consciousness.

As you open to experiencing yourself as a new thing, you will begin to experience yourself seeing new things as more unified, awakening to the presence of the *holy* in everyday life. You will become more interested in being both a passive presence and an active presence for unifying things around you into wholeness. While holiness and wholeness are one, holiness is a word seemingly owned by the religious realm. I suggest that we reclaim it as a word for everyday use. Joining with that which is holy is more easily accomplished when we have an internal perception of ourselves as whole—a perception our souls provide for us.

From this place of interconnectedness, we can offer our time in service to help create a more nonviolent, peaceful world—this is what I refer to as "soulful society." We can also offer our time in spiritual practice within communities, whether through shamanic states or yoga or meditation, to extend healing and peace and love to the broader community. This practice begins internally, with the soul, and then moves out into the larger world through words or actions. These are prayers for peace, meditations of love, intentions for specific nonviolence and world peace. Often, these goals of the Soul Realm will become a natural interest and preoccupation once your soul is awakened within your own body. As you begin to experience the presence of your uniqueness of soul, all that is holy, the Soul Realm will inform your ethics and guide your actions. As you experience more inner light and love, you will find yourself extending this light and love out into the world. As stated in the Bible, "Love never fails" (1 Corinthians 13:8);

love can prevail if we allow its force to win out. This is not meant to be simplistic at all.

When we contemplate the power of hatred to feed wars and violence, we must remember that the force of love is so much more powerful than hatred. Therefore, we want to try to remember to cultivate love in all circumstances. This keeps the flame of the heart lit, fostering more love and light in the world. Regardless of external circumstances and conflicts, which are real, your soul is here to remind you that you can be guided by an ethic of love and be interested in seeing its power prevail over other, darker forces. Remember the complex, ancient myth of Eros and Psyche—Love and the Soul—in which the soul winds through many trials and tribulations, ultimately reconnecting, fruitfully and fulfilling, with its own initiation into full maturity of knowing: oneness with Love is all there is.

CHAPTER 9
ANCIENT SYMBOLS TO HELP YOU ON YOUR JOURNEY

The following ancient healing symbols are particularly powerful in reconstructing and reconfiguring the internal space into a unified whole, all essential as healing catalysts when one is working with addictions and other psychic inertias. Soul retrieval is essential in accessing lost parts of self. Fragmented aspects of self and soul can unify only from the inside out, nurturing deliberate acts to reclaim soul's purpose and conscious awareness of enlightened health. When these symbols appear to do their work, relax and enjoy the power of their healing medicine.

Ancient, Sacred Symbols of Spiritual Awakening

Symbols of spiritual awakening often manifest themselves in natural phenomena in the world, reminding us of the power of Spirit to transform into matter. These occurrences remind us that Spirit does, in fact, want to disclose itself through matter. Nature reminds us by the day, through the solar cycle, of the vastness and majesty of Creation. The continual cycles of the solstices and the equinoxes, or the lunar cycle, the waxing and waning of the moon's presence, all function as spiritual supports for our material life. For the ancients, the constant repetition of the symbols was the assurance of the spirits' unfailing presence. Their presence meant that a distinctly divine consciousness was gradually coming to reign over humanity, a kingdom of goodness, truth, and beauty; a kingdom of love. There are archetypal symbols and primary beings I especially want to highlight so that if they appear in your meditations, you will be able to recognize them and respond:

1. **Jesus, the Great Shaman, the Christos.** Many experience this being as the divine soul of every human being. This being deepens our understanding of the embodiment of Christ consciousness. This is

very simply the magnetic core, the healing energy of the Son/sun, where our solar plexus opens like an umbrella and expands, radiating light and love into every crevice of our being. Christ often appears knocking on the door of our hearts, which can be viewed as unlocking the dusty chambers of the heart space, where we often bury old pain and grief, consequently shutting down to the giving and receiving of the transformative power of unconditional love in our lives. Whenever this figure in white appears, there are always beautiful lessons in love, truth, and awakening to personal strength and power—the opening of the chambers of the heart vibration recalibrate the heart to the deeper language of love. In the New Testament, we are reminded by Jesus that "the Kingdom of God is within you" (Luke 17:21). Jesus's life on earth was the model for us of the integration of Divinity and humanity and the opportunity, as humans, to choose the divine path of love. If you have roots in a Christian tradition, the ascended Jesus may appear to you regularly, to feed the internal explosion of a feminine/masculine balanced energy that radiates at a higher, holy frequency of supernatural love. This presence of love usually appears as a light form, awakening us to the purity of truth and beauty as a supernatural force that heals.

2. **Crow, or Raven.** Known as "the shamanic surgeon" or "the messenger in the mystical world," this great shape-shifter helps us "shift and lift," bringing change in consciousness, increased self-knowledge, and introspective reflection. Crow will "dismember to re-member," often tearing apart or ripping out that which must go in order to create anew; Crow is not always gentle and kind while the work is being done, but you can trust that the end result, the "re-membering"—or reconfiguring—will be peaceful and calming. Crow replaces the death layer with renewed, fresh energies—new cognition, new affect states, and a new skill set for new behaviors—helping transform and guide you into greater wholeness and new dimensions in your healing process. Its "caw-caw" is the call to awaken into that deeper reality, that hidden consciousness that awaits our response. I remember the session when my client Rachel, as I was drumming for her during a

therapeutic session, felt a horrific pain in her heart. She described it as her "old heart of stone" being torn out and being replaced with a "new heart of unconditional love." She actually felt this in her body in a visceral way and experienced herself, afterwards, moving through the world in a more openhearted manner, connecting in a new way with a healthy self-love, which naturally radiated out to the larger world. This more pure love for herself enabled Rachel to love others with greater acceptance and compassion and less judgment, allowing for greater enjoyment in the intimate relationships of her life. While this may sound simplistic and cause you to be skeptical, *it is important to remember that this practice is a mystico-magical one and must be experienced first-hand to be more fully understood and perceived as credible.*

3. **The Serpent of Transmutation.** This being helps us shed that which must go, reminding us that life is about acceptance of change and embrace of surrender. Radical acceptance of that which is unfolding right before our eyes often holds our soul's potentiality, unfolding. Serpent is the creature that supports our release, our letting go, our surrender into our soul's ascension. The serpent often appears coiled in the base of the spine, then travels up the spine, indicating that the kundalini (or chi), the life-force energy, is being awakened and is rising. There will be an internal experience of old layers shedding and literally dropping off, often from the shoulders, melting into the ground of earth—or perhaps being carried away by the River of Life. When this healing medicine arises, your spine will usually feel sturdier. You will experience more backbone as your back body more steadily supports your front body. Many clients have expressed feeling this backbone—their back body— supporting their front body in powerful new ways. This awakening of courageous and willful energies will offer greater strength, insight, and connection to one's truth and clarity of purpose, as the "dragon tail" within lengthens and supports the internal structure. Remembering the shamanic model, wherein we are constantly being dismembered to be re-membered into new birth of new being is essential. In this circular, repetitive act—the spiral—we are always seeking to remember more and more of our soul's knowing, no

longer wandering aimlessly, without purpose, while at the same time releasing and surrendering what is no longer needed so that it may be transformed in service to Spirit. Our soul desires that we know our purpose and fulfill our destiny in this lifetime. The serpent is the magico-mystical, transformational creature that supports congruence, moving the body and soul into aligned action of soul's calling. Tragically, whether intentionally or otherwise, the sacred Christian text (the Bible) opens its storytelling with an often demonized depiction of this powerful transmutational spirit helper. Our awakening to the healing powers of this being requires us to unlearn and release the twisted, pathologized image of this spirit friend. Like many of the other ancient symbols of healing and power, its meaning has been reversed, over time, to mask its transformative powers for good.

4. **Ceremonial Mask (often of a bird) and Feathered or Fabric Robe.** In soul-retrieval work, when we are initiated into greater depths of seeing into the dark or are being elevated to a higher frequency as one with Soul, we often receive a ceremonial mask and robe, usually with feathers. We then receive a vision of ourselves with a new head and a renewed body: new eyes to see, new ears to hear, and new, light body (feathers) to vibrate at a higher frequency (the feathers are usually fluttering in magical flight). This imagery symbolizes the awakening of renewed perception and an opening to new affect states of good feeling or lightness of being. A robe of feathers from a winged creature will usually appear, signifying a renewed cloaking of this lightness of being and an ability to traverse the two worlds of earth and sky with new vision. The physical realm and the Divine Realm will function in a more unified manner and with greater ease, not being so weighted down by life's trials and tribulations. Once the mask and robe have been conferred, the image may morph into an image of self as a tree, the renewed self as the Tree of Life, rooted in earth, open to sky.

5. **The River of Life.** This image will often appear, symbolizing the water element's medicinal qualities gently prodding us (sometimes pushing us) toward forward movement—always cleansing and

purifying into greater translucence, ease, and clarity of purpose. This is a visual reminder that, daily, we are being carried by this River of Life throughout the trials and challenges of our existence. This river also reminds us that as we align ourselves with the flow of life, there is a certain right rhythm to our soul's unraveling. We will find ourselves in our soul's knowing, which will foster an internal confidence and assurance, throughout the passage of time; this confidence carries intrinsically a certain flow, a fluidity—a trust in the movement of life. The water element is interested in our soul's purification, removing that which must go to make way for the new. This is how we reach our soul's pure potentiality. This water element may also show itself as a waterfall caressing through the crown of your head or perhaps as the sea swirling inside you and around you. Water will morph into its many different forms, teaching you that you, too, can practice morphing with the movement of life. When you see this water element, be sure to awaken consciously to its powerful medicine, remembering that the River of Life is always the reminder of the presence of the mystical power answering back to the River of Forgetfulness.

6. **The Infinity Symbol.**

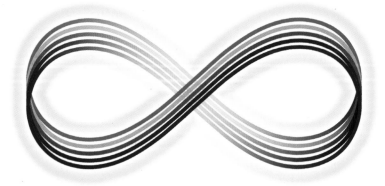

Signs and symbols have always been fundamental means of delivering particular messages. The symbol of Infinity, also called the "lemniscate," universally represents eternity, the numinous and higher spiritual powers. Rudolph Steiner, the founder of anthroposophy, worked with the lemniscate, as did Plato, who describes this symbol in *The Timaeus*. St. Thomas Aquinas, also referencing the lemniscate's healing powers, equated its energies to the circular movement of angels. Often this symbol initially appears with a figure-eight movement that morphs into a circular or spiral motion or form, in the core area of the solar plexus (after moving from north to south, earth to sky, then east to west, arm to arm). Its primary function is to integrate the polarities of self and disowned dualities of soul into greater union within the body, so that the self is not working against the soul. Without internal unification, confusion abounds. Internal conflict fosters a restless spirit—this is not the holding ground for inner peace.

Infinity's medicine unifies the sacred feminine and sacred masculine, internally, usually beginning at the soles of the feet and spreading up to the crown through the breath, south to north. Through this medicine, you will be internally restored to your natural rhythm, experiencing greater balance and internal wholeness. This experience will foster good feeling and nurture an inner calm, allowing easier access to your personal power from an inner core of strength. The infinity symbol also appears to mend the five body splits discussed in chapter 1, assisting in healing old psychological wounds from trauma and abuse, body divisions, and disconnects between the head and the heart or the root sacrum and perhaps the upper body. When the infinity symbol arrives in your inner vision, the flow of the breath will be strengthened and you will feel as though your body is being gently rocked by something bigger than you. The tenderness of the rocking motion will help create greater internal peace from within; often tears flow as the healing medicine takes effect. Allow this symbol to work its transformative medicine; surrendering to its magic and embracing its flow is key. These energies will move you into deeper relaxation, and you will feel extremely restored as you are moved from darkness and ignorance into light and understanding. You may even begin to shake and tremble as your body releases old energies that need to go. When you feel complete, be sure to thank this symbol and acknowledge your awareness of its healing presence. Learn to work with it and dialogue with it as if it were your beloved friend—because it is. The mantra *Sat nam,* which means, "My true identity is infinity," is a very common mantra chanted in many yoga classes. *Sat* means "essence" or "truth," while *nam* means "name" or "identity." The soul's true identity is rooted in this knowing or recognition of itself as *Infinity*. When this symbol has successfully completed its medicine, this recognition will come instinctively.

7. **The Healing Wan/Svastika, or the Sacred Symbol of the X.** This symbol represents an incredibly powerful, ancient healing *force*. In China, it is called the *wan*. In Sanskrit, the word is *svastika*. The word "swastika" comes from the Sanskrit "svastika"— *su* meaning "good," *asti* meaning "to be," and *ka* as a suffix. The wan/svastika has been used by many cultures throughout the past three thousand years to represent

Photo taken from the wall of an Indian Ashram in Rishikesh, India

the restorative life force, the healing rays of the powerful sun, and the healing energies of balance, strength, and abundance. Within the oral tradition of many healing traditions, the wan/svastika is still a sacred symbol, with positive connotations and powerful influence; it often appears in the ethereal realm and imprints forcefully into the solar plexus, unifying the sacred masculine and sacred feminine in greater balance and personal power. This symbol in its pure form has nothing to do with the Nazis' evil doings. In fact, quite the contrary is true. Cross-culturally, this ancient healing symbol represents love as a force: a force that unifies, a force that empowers, a force that feeds balance, a force of Divinity. It was due to the evil force of darkness that this symbol was twisted and used as a force of evil, forever poisoning the purity of the symbol's power to heal. This is an absolute distortion of its original intent, which seeks restoration and clarification.

Like an axe, this medicinal X consistently works in the core, restoring balance to the center of the solar plexus, where the soul's will and power to act are centered. The svatiska symbol, tainted for too long by its appropriation by the Nazis, was found in ancient Hindu, Mexican, and Buddhist traditions, and many others. The name comes from the Sanskrit world and refers to a mystical cross denoting good fortune. Some authorities say it was meant to represent the sun with its rays. Repeatedly, to my ongoing amazement, many clients have told me that they feel the force of this symbol—and they see it in their inner vision before I mention it to them—a force not unlike the branding of a cow. Often this symbol shows itself in the color of midnight black, reminding us of the darkness of the creative force moving toward an awakening into the light—the rebirth from nothingness into creation, from forgetting to remembering. Sometimes, this symbol appears in the beginning of a session and sometimes the symbol enters at the end of a session, after other soul beings have worked their healing. Again, whenever it appears, offer thanks and gratitude for its healing, balancing, and stabilizing presence. This symbol helps us restore the body from disorientation and fragmentation.

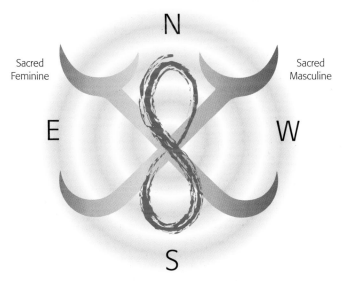

Healing Energy imprints from the core and vibrates out.

Ancient healing symbol, wan/svastika. Works in conjunction with infinity symbol as Medicine.

This healing symbol brands itself through the *center* of the solar plexus, radiating energy out, as a black chromosomal X with little half-moons on the tip of each X end, radiating from the internal core, out into the world.

As we work repeatedly in shamanic states of consciousness, we learn that repeated exposure decreases sensitization (in psychological terms). *So what does this mean to you?* The more you experience the power of each ancient symbol to heal and each soul helper to reconstruct, the more you will enjoy the effects of the inner work as your skepticism, reluctance, and doubt are washed away. Authentic change and inner harmony begin first from within, in our inside body. As we connect with our breath, we begin to experience our inner structure moving in a rhythmic motion, like an ocean wave, from north to south, east to west. Eventually, this life force will move in all four directions, then in a circular motion—like the sun or the moon or the drum. Often the svastika symbol forms the circle on the top half and the circle on the bottom half, as if the upper world meets the lower world through the circle of union (in our solar plexus). As we learn to balance these elements in our bodies, experiencing more balance and personal power, we naturally move out into the larger world to create communities that balance shared power. Our inner world reflects out onto the larger environmental field as we foster domination-free orders—soulful communities rooted in mutual respect, equality, compassion, and unconditional love.

The fruit of the righteous is a Tree of Life (James 3:17)

8. **The Tree of Life.** The Tree of Life is symbolic in many different spiritual traditions, displaying its roots spreading deep into the earth and its branches reaching to the sky, uniting the heavens and the earth in ideal balance. This is believed to be opening communication between the cosmic planes (between earth and heaven), "making possible ontological passage from one mode of being to another. It is such a break in the heterogeneity of profane space that creates the center through which communication with the transmundane is established."[1] This very visual reminder—like gifts in nature all around us—awakens

us to the possibility *in our bodies* of internal unification and connect-edness with both the heavens (the Soul Realm, at the crown) and the earth (the root chakra). To be rooted in both the earth and the sky allows us to be grounded in a solid foundational way while still opening to transcendence and expansiveness, which is consistently our next new layer of unfolding growth: our soul's ascension. Once you become comfortable with connecting earth to sky within the con-tainer of your body, you will begin to feel the flow of your own breath moving from north to south, connecting you with an internal rocking. This energetic movement helps feed the attachment with your soul's vibration. The breath often begins to move in a circular direction, feeling as though the moon or the sun is circling inside you, initially localized in your solar plexus, and then circling all around you, moving in concentric circles outside your energy field. When you begin to feel this vibration, learn to surrender to it, almost as if you were on a float in the ocean, moving to the wavelike, rocking motion of the sea. These are the unifying energies of soul, connecting you with your life-force energy, which connects you with universal energies, larger and more expansive than you. This is the experience of soul meeting Cosmic Soul.

Consistent with this teaching is the legend of *The Emerald Tablet*, said to have been discovered in a caved tomb, clutched in the hands of the corpse of Hermes Trismegistus. In it was written: "*Know then the Greatest Secret of the Universe: As above, so below—As within, so without.*"

9. **Sun and Moon Consciousness Integrated Within.** The ancient symbol of the healing wan/svastika is a balancing medicine of the sacred: sun consciousness, which embodies the right side of the body (the masculine), and moon consciousness, which embodies the left side of the body (the feminine). While this symbol is applying its medicine, these energies are being fully balanced and integrated in the internal body structure, filling the inner body, from the inside out, with a radiant light. As you learn to balance these polarities, such as action/inaction, expression/silence, movement/stillness, play/form, et cetera, you will begin to experience a greater calm and inner strength of power. This ancient healing symbol, appearing

like a chromosomal X with a circle around the center, almost like the image of the Celtic cross, will sometimes forcefully imprint its medicine in an incredibly visceral way. This healing energy penetrates the core of the solar plexus, then travels north to south, from crown to root, then east to west, fingertip to fingertip of each hand, penetrating the heart, circling from the center, vibrating out from the core, into every cell, every fiber of internal space. Similar to the awakening force of the kundalini energy in Hinduism, or the baptism of the Holy Spirit in Christianity, this intense medicine is experienced physically. You may also witness colors or see flowers. Again, each color is at work to heal the particular energy center of the chakra system, like the colors of the rainbow. You may see red (root chakra); orange (sacral chakra); yellow (solar plexus); green or fuscia (heart chakra); blue (throat chakra); indigo (third eye); or white, gold, or purple (crown chakra). Trust that each of these colors is applying its medicine to heighten your inner body's balance and openness. Once this is complete, you will begin to experience yourself as a "light" body—lighter, with a heightened awareness of looking at yourself and your life through the lens of enlightenment.

As we learn to trust this process of being reconfigured in these physical bodies as human spirits, we trust that each healing symbol and soul helper is integrating and balancing our internal physical body, our *human* self, with our *spiritual* body, our unified soul. This internal balance allows us to move powerfully in groundedness of earth (physical body) with expansive sky (spiritual self). Our repeated contact with the unseen universe, through a daily spiritual practice, allows us to more deeply understand that we are spirits having a human experience and not the other way around. Our souls fully understand that the circumstances of our lives can be understood and perceived differently than through the lens of the wounded personality. The Soul Realm will reveal itself to us on a regular basis and work its magic, if we allow ourselves to remain receptive to the information. All the healing symbols discussed in this book are committed to our unification, wholeness, and reinstitution of inner balance. Become acquainted with this one, the Hindu svastika, in particular, as it is your friend. Please don't allow history to distort the truth of its sacred purity. In the same way that we work to retrieve the purity of our own souls, the purity of this sacred symbol also seeks restoration to its original form.

10. **Power Animals as Soul Protectors.** Shamanic methodology is rooted in the belief that each of us has soul protectors who appear through visitations as power animals or spirit helpers. In your inner vision and your internal cylinder, while in shamanic states, you will often see many of these medicinal symbols working in conjunction with one another, as they instinctively know exactly what is needed for your internal body to heal. Again, the Soul Realm is an inclusive and cooperative community that works collaboratively—as if demonstrating for us humans how systems function best. Additionally, you will begin to know each of your soul protectors over time and understand that sometimes they change, depending on what is needed for each phase of your journey. Be patient. I have been practicing since 1996, and just recently, within the last several years, I have been seeing more and more faces of "the faceless ones." Sometimes these protectors change or morph throughout our life cycle, depending on what particular medicine we need.

I still remember the day when, working with a Reiki colleague/ friend very deeply, I had my first experience at seeing for myself my own power animals, which had lived in my body for a very long time. I saw very clearly the jaguar, which lives in the left side of my body and had been there as my soul protector since I was a little girl. And on the right side of my body was my white horse, like Pegasus, protecting the sacred masculine's development in my body.

As a girl I aligned myself primarily with masculine energies, as I had two older brothers whom I adored and a strong, masculine father whom I revered and respected. Clearly, as a young and vulnerable girl, I modeled the masculine way of moving through the world because in my family of origin it appeared to hold greater power. My daddy used to affectionately refer to me as the "bucking bronco that needed to be tamed." Now I understand more fully that this animal (horse) was, and still is, my soul's protector. It was horse energy as well as my soul's essence that my dad was encountering and labeling as "bucking bronco." Additional power animals have been with me for a very long time and I trust will continue to be—as is true for you.

The cougar (who also morphs into jaguar, cheetah, and lioness), existing among the cat family, devotedly abides with me, as was true for the women warriors of the ancient feminine tradition. For example, Durga, the Hindu goddess warrior, travels with her lion. And in many of the ancient hieroglyphics you will see the goddesses with one of the cats by their side. In many ancient spiritual traditions, the cat family (jaguars, cheetahs, lions, and cougars) represent the keepers of the sacred feminine mysteries, also known as the wise woman tradition. At Halloween, the black cat is still perceived as the symbol of the creature that travels the night sky with the healer witches. These were the female healers taking magical flight, traversing the dark, fertile void, who opposed traditional religious dogma, magically curing with their pagan healing potions. Now I see and more fully understand how these two beautiful creatures (jaguar and horse) protected me and my soul throughout my lifetime; on many days, I am overwhelmed with gratitude because their protective presence is so real.

Know that you have your own *designated* soul protectors as well and that each spirit being is eager for you to recognize its medicinal presence in your life. It is believed, in the shamanic tradition, that if you do not recognize them, they will most likely leave. This would be a huge loss for you, so please, dialogue with them. Go bravely inside to receive this wealth of information that awaits your attention.

In shamanic practice, your soul guides and animal helpers will be working in conjunction with the ancient symbols to bring healing medicine to foster your internal unification and wholeness. As we become more whole on the inside, we no longer have the need to act out disowned parts of self on the external environment. As we come home to these bodily containers, we move, gently and with loving compassion, into the spaces of these wounded internal body splits, always bringing our conscious breath into the tight spots, offering love and compassion to the wounded self. Working with the elemental breaths of earth, water, fire, air, and ether, we begin to engage these powerful healing energies, infusing our bodies with the healing powers from the soul. Each time, these divine beings, soul helpers, and elemental medicinal images will work their transformative magic—known as "extraction work" in shamanic terms—specific to what is needed, creating fluidity and flow with the natural rhythm of connection with our soul in the internal body.

These symbols and beings all resonate at the frequency of the Soul Realm, a vibration very different from when we are living in the fears, anxieties, or worries of this human experience. The divine order of things constantly seeks to answer back (within our bodymind) to the chaos and confusion of this earthly realm. As we practice listening and seeing from the inside out, we will begin to understand this new heartbeat. The consistent beat of the frame drum can hold the space for the heart to open. The consistent drumbeat tethers us to the beat of the soul.

EPILOGUE

CULTIVATING AN INTENTIONAL, INTEGRAL, TRANSFORMATIONAL COMMUNITY—THE GLOBAL WORLD

We're all just walking each other home.

RAM DASS

O nce you've created an experience of establishing psychological safety in your own body—body as holy temple / safe container— you will be rooted and expansive in your soul's expression. The characteristics of soul will foster an unconditional love with an open heart that feeds authenticity and vulnerability; this will feed compassion, tolerance, and impartiality within the larger systems of your world. As you continue to heal from the inside out, you will naturally seek to bring this internal, unified whole out into the external world. Thomas Merton refers to this as *"being an obedient instrument of a transcendent will."* Through the development of the gifts of your soul, along with feedback and confirmation from your local soulful community about being seen in your giftedness, your actions will organically lead to contribution and service to the broader community. The purpose of doing this healing work of attachment with our soul is not only for our own healing but for the global healing of the Cosmic Soul's intention, a compassionate and connected larger world. We will find ourselves intentionally seeking out and growing communities that embrace authentic soul expression. These communities will naturally support *an ethic of justice and unification* as a natural, organic repercussion of doing this soulful practice, as these are the qualities of a soul consciousness. As the inner splits and self-alienation are healed, an inner cosmic dynamism will result. Like bees who live and work in community to produce honey, we will learn to live and work together harmoniously to end divisions, supporting justice, nonviolence, and the sweetness of life for all—in the name of Love.

QUALITIES OF SOUL CONSCIOUSNESS

> *But the wisdom from above is first pure then peaceable, gentle, reasonable, full of mercy and good fruits unwavering without hypocrisy. And the seed whose fruit is righteousness is sown in peace by those who make peace.*
>
> JAMES 3:17

❖ **Purity**: The enlightened consciousness informed by unconditional love and purity of heart

❖ **Clarity**: Inner peace quiets the inner restlessness and lights the path to clarity of soul's consciousness

❖ **Right Action**: External behaviors are aligned with an expansive, open heart fostering congruence in thought and action

The compassionate teachings of the Buddha remind us to "light the lamp within; strive hard to attain wisdom. Become pure and innocent, and live in the world of light." ("On Impurity," *The Dhammapada*, ed. Eknath Easwaran, 194.). Jesus and many other holy teachers have encouraged us to do the same. Purity, innocence, and light are characteristics of one who is infused by soul.

As you practice these principles more and more in your daily life, you will begin to notice how at home you feel with the like-minded people you call "constructive community." As you practice nurturing an experience of embodiment of soul, both locally and globally, you will begin to witness the content of this book functioning daily as a living, active devotional meditation. Each of us is better enabled to put our bodies and our souls into "right action" within compassionate, soulful communities (as opposed to disembodied, cut-off communities where members are in role). Daily effort and commitment to this practice is essential so that we can familiarize ourselves with attachment to our own soul. The more we do this as a daily discipline, the more we will be able to distinguish when we are feeling attached to our soul and when we are not. As the Rev. Dr. Serene Jones said in her delivery of a prayer for the nation at the Fifty-seventh Presidential Inaugural Prayer Service, we are called to "put our bodies and souls in motion in the spirit of our brother Martin [Luther King, Jr.], on behalf of the poor and disenfranchised, the worn and the weary, the bruised and the afflicted." Practice living with intentional interconnectedness as you observe how each person's gifts and talents affect the others. Notice in your own body how the big toe affects the entire foot and the how the hand is connected to the heart. A constructive, compassionate community works the same way. We are deeply interconnected, and the energy of one affects the energy of another. We want to be in communities that help us cultivate the energies of soul: purity, peacefulness, and right action.

As we deepen in our own understanding of how profoundly we each affect the other, there is an attunement that occurs as we learn to "tune in" to that which fosters our soul's aliveness and that which deadens it. As we learn to live in a way that shows deep respect for soul activity and for how connected we truly are, we will begin to offer one another greater graciousness and kindness and love. As you learn to feed your natural instinct of belonging with the broader community (allow it to feel good), your soul's expression will shine through and the community will positively affirm your uniqueness. As you are nurturing your own open heart, you will naturally create and foster open systems wherever you go, as you support others in their freedom of authentic soul's expression and inclusion of differences—even differing belief systems become the ground for curious conversations and growth. Notice with awareness and without judgment when you begin to contract while living with an open heart in community. Learn to honor both your contraction and your expansion, like the breath of life. In this way, you allow yourself to move toward contact and away from contact (withdrawal). Both polarities of the contact/withdrawal cycle are valuable when one is living in a community of wounded humans, fostering the practical experiment of the application of soul principles to relationships. Honoring contact and withdrawal allows time for reflection and stillness when necessary, fostering balance and wholeness and love. The community effectively becomes the place where we are given a second chance, to try again, to learn to love better and respond with more wisdom, feeding the nurturing of each soul in its ascension.

While living in community (your primary community may be the people you share a house or an office with, or it may be your local church or synagogue or yoga community), observe both yourself and others, supporting yourself in the freedom to be your soul's embodiment while you practice tolerance and love, extending the same to others. You just may begin to see other souls unveiling themselves before you. Be brave and become an active participant in others' soul edification. Practice engagement of the questions about soul and discussions about the Holy Mystery as a matter of conversation. Practice tolerance toward those systems and individuals that dogmatically prescribe answers in a manner that is limiting and constrictive. Send love, light, and healing, moment to moment, out into the broader world (envisioning this from your internal third eye); especially practice graciousness in the intimate relationships of your life. Seek to find and align yourself with those communities whose expressed values you resonate with. Ideally, as we create a more open internal spaciousness and live connected to the Mystery of our souls in our bodies, we will then cultivate that open space in the larger world. As the inner reality is constantly emanating vibrational repercussions into the external, environmental field, we remember to each reach out into the world with the values and characteristics of the Cosmic Soul: love, truth, purity, harmony, balance, and beauty.

As systems theory affirms, the system changes one member at a time. As each of us changes from the inside out, committed to healing our own internal fragmentation, dichotomies (body splits), and soul loss, perhaps then the world will better be able to move away from such deep division and into greater harmony and unification. This will happen naturally and organically as we get better at caring tenderly for each other and all living creatures, including the earth. Only from an internal experience of wholeness will we be able to then extend this sense of wholeness to others as we remember that the state of our internal world becomes what we project out onto others.

ENGAGEMENT IN PERSONAL AND SOCIAL TRANSFORMATION

Through the reading of this book and the application of its tools, may the lamp within be lit—because we know how to light it—and may the light that shines in the midst of the darkness begin to shine brighter inside each one of us—because we know how to nurture it. As we now practice daily nurturing this light, may our individual intention and commitment to the path of soul retrieval and soul embodiment have a healing, communal impact on the larger global world, supporting all living creatures in a life connected to the heartbeat of soul—the true interconnectedness. As we do the daily work to heal ourselves, becoming more whole from the inside out, may we each naturally and organically move outward into the larger community, to extend healing and wholeness to the global "body." As we understand that these efforts are simply a by-product of our internal process, we will effect planetary healing as the larger Cosmic Soul is retrieved and unified, one individual soul at a time.

ACKNOWLEDGMENTS
Many Thanks for the Journey

I have gathered these morsels shared here mainly through my own shamanic practice, as well as experiences shared with my fellow pilgrims along the way and my psychotherapy clients, to whom I am forever grateful. My precious clients have trusted me and invited me to share my shamanic insights with them, session after session, for almost seventeen years. I have devoured just about everything written about the soul from many different spiritual traditions. For fourteen years, I met every month with other New Jersey ministers, psychotherapists, and shamanic practitioners. Calling ourselves the Owl Women, we integrated Christian principles and Christian mysticism with shamanism, working mainly with Jesus as the Great Shaman, the healing medicine of White Owl, and many of the Christian mystics. In 1997, I trained with Michael Harner in core shamanism and furthered my training with the shamans of Mexico and the Medicine Fox Sisters of North and South Dakota.

I am grateful I was given the opportunity in 2008 to run therapeutic groups for Princeton House Behavioral Health. Their progressive psychiatrists and enlightened clinical directors asked me to facilitate spirituality groups using my frame drum. Since the groups were both didactic and experiential in nature, most of what I shared was the content of this book. There I was, banging my drum with the chronic mentally ill and the dually diagnosed / chemically addicted patients whom I grew to love. So many of them, to whom I am also eternally grateful, inspired both my brain and my spirit for two solid years. Their encouraging feedback helped strengthen my belief in this work in my times of doubt and skepticism. I thank each one of them for their support and the lessons they taught me about the value of shamanism in the therapeutic setting. Much to my surprise, this group became a favorite of many patients and therapists, who reported that it fostered the patient's increase in mood stability, therapeutic insight, and an expanded self-love. I believe these are the signs of the presence of the soul living as one with the body.

I am thankful to my dear friends Felicia Norton and Charles Smith, who coauthored the book *An Emerald Earth: Cultivating a Natural Spirituality & Serving Beauty in Our World*. Through sharing many spiritual circles with them and cultivating my spiritual practice, I became immersed in the value of elemental breath work as a way of affirming our rootedness in the sacredness of life. It is essential to both ground and root before traveling into communion with the Ethereal Realm. Before them, Sufi teacher Hazrat Inayat Khan, the founder of the Sufi Order in the West in 1910 and teacher of Universal Sufism and the profound Ziraat teachings, was also a great teacher of the five elements including ether.

Many thanks for the devoted attention and perceptive feedback given to me through multiple iterations by both Deborah Tesser and Marion Reinson.

Mostly, though, I am profoundly grateful to my clients, whose daily persistence, curiosity and wonder supported me in exploring, even growing to worship, the breadth and depth of the integrated soul guides discovered through the shamanic path. And my one client, in particular, on the brink of suicide, who allowed herself to be dragged up repeatedly from the bottom of the sea by whale medicine, eventually emerging into her soul's full glory. You know who you are, and I will forever treasure the gift, far greater than gold, of the years we shared in sacred discovery. May this book awaken you to the possibility of your soul's knowing as your most holy guide for daily living.

Endnotes

PREFACE

1. William James, *The Varieties of Religious Experience* (New York: Barnes & Noble Classics, 2004), p. 61.
2. Donald Kalsched is a clinical psychologist and Jungian psychoanalyst who has written extensively on early trauma and disassociation theory: *The Inner World of Trauma: Archetypal Defences of the Personal Spirit* (East Sussex, UK: Routledge, 1996).
3. See C. G. Jung, *Mysterium Coniunctionis, Collected Works*, vol. 14 (Princeton, NJ: Princeton University Press, 1989), p. 180.
4. Jalal al-Din Rumi, Cited in Joel Levey and Michelle Levy, *Simple Meditation and Relaxation* (Berkeley, CA: Conari Press, 1999), p. 234.
5. Plato, *The Republic of Plato*, "Book X." Translated by Allan Bloom (New York: Basic Books, 1991).
6. Swami Brahmdev, *Questions and Answers* (Uttrakhand, India: Aurovalley Ashram, 2006), p. 47.

INTRODUCTION

1. Harris Poll, "What People Do and Do Not Believe In," (http://www.harrisinteractive.com/vault/Harris_Poll_2009_12_15.pdf).
2. Pew Research Poll, "18% of Americans say they've seen a ghost," http://www.pewresearch.orgfact-tank/2013/10/30/18-of-americans-say-theyve-seen-a-ghost/
3. Thomas Merton, "The Significance of the Bhagavad Gita," Introduction to *The Bhagavad-Gita As It Is* by A.C. Bhaktivedanta Swami Prabhupada (New York: Macmillan, 1968).

CHAPTER I

1. Frederick Perls, *Gestalt Therapy Verbatim* (Gouldsboro, ME: The Gestalt Journal Press, 1992).
2. Ken Dychtwald, *BodyMind* (New York: Tarcher-Putnam, 1986).

3. Mircea Eliade, *Shamanism: Archaic Techniques of Ecstasy* (Princeton, NJ: Princeton University Press, 1964), p. 8).

4. Alberto Villoldo, *Shaman, Healer, Sage: How to Heal Yourself and Others with the Energy Medicine of the Americas* (New York: Harmony Books, 2000).

5. C. G. Jung, *Mysterium Coniunctionis*, p. 365: "The alchemists, who in their own way knew more about the nature of the individuation process than we moderns do, expressed this paradox through the symbol of the ouroboros, the snake that eats its own tail. In the age-old image of the ouroboros lies the thought of devouring oneself and turning oneself into a circulatory process, for it was clear to the more astute alchemists that the prima materia of the art was man himself. The ouroboros is a dramatic symbol for the integration and assimilation of the opposite, i.e. of the shadow. This 'feed-back' process is at the same time a symbol of immortality, since it is said of the ouroboros that he slays himself and brings himself to life, fertilizes himself and gives birth to himself. He symbolizes the One, who proceeds from the clash of opposites, and he therefore constitutes the secret of the prima materia which [. . .] unquestionably stems from man's unconscious."

6. Mircea Eliade, *The Sacred and Profane: The Nature of Religion* (New York: Harcourt, 1987), pg. 11).

CHAPTER 2

1. Meister Eckhart, *Selected Treatises and Sermons*, trans. J. M. Clark and J. V. Skinner (London: Fount, 1994), p. 167.

2. Cited in Jean Varenne, *Yoga and the Hindu Tradition*, translated by Derek Coleman (New Delhi: Motilal Barnarsidass, 1989), p. 57.

3. Hank Wesselman, *Medcinemaker: Mystic Encounters Along the Shaman's Path* (New York: Bantam Books, 1998).

4. Joseph Campbell, *The Hero with a Thousand Faces* (Novato, CA: New World Library), p. 64ff.

5. Mircea Eliade, *The Sacred and Profane, p. 13*

CHAPTER 3

1. *Tom Harpur, The Pagan Christ: Is Blind Faith Killing Christianity?* (New York: Walker & Company, 2004), p. 35.

2. William Wordsworth, *The Poems of William Wordsworth* (London: Metheun & Co., 1908). P. 27.

3. Cited in Tom Harpur, *The Pagan Christ*, p. 41.

4. Saint Augstine, cited in ibid., p. 27.

5. Jalal al-Din Rumi, *The Essential Rumi*, translated by Coleman Barks (New York: Penguin Books, 1999), p. 109.

6. Jesus's life on this earth is a great example of this fully human / fully divine embodiment. From what we can access of the historical account, Jesus's human struggle was with divine purpose, yet the spiritual transcended.

7. Wilhelm Reich, *The Function of the Orgasm: Sex-economic problems of biological energy* (London: Panther, 1968), p. 362.

8. Jalal al-Din Rumi, cited in Jonathan H. Ellerby, *Return to the Sacred: Ancient Pathways to Spiritual Awakening* (Carlsbad, CA: Hay House, 2010), p. 232.

9. Penina V. Adelman, "Before" from *Gates to the New City: A Treasury of Modern Jewish Tales*, edited by Howard Schwartz. Northvale, NJ: Jason Aronson Inc., 1991.

CHAPTER 4

1. Many of the great, powerful goddesses, cross-culturally, are seen in graphic images with the serpent, owls, and the cat family. On Sekhmet, see Robert Masters, *The Goddess Sekhmet: Psycho-Spiritual Exercises of the Fifth Way* (Ashland, OR: White Cloud Press, 2002).

2. John Philip Newell, "Our Oldest Unity," http://heartbeatjourney. org/2014/05/23our-oldest-unity-john-philip-newell-isle-of-iona-new-harmony/

3. This simple elemental breath work can be done in the morning before you get out of bed, in the evening before falling into sleep, or sitting at your desk, you can pause and come into the balancing of these energies through breath.

CHAPTER 5

1. Plato, *Protagoras*, translated by Benjamin Jowett (Rockville, MD: Serenity Publishers, 2009), p. 29.

2. Eckhart Tolle, *The Power of Now: A Guide to Spiritual Enlightenment* (Novato, CA: New World Library, 1999).

3.   Mircea Eliade, *The Sacred and the Profane*, pp. 68-69.

4.   Cited in Tabatha Yeatts, *Albert Einstein* (New York: Sterling Publishing, 2007), p. 116.

CHAPTER 6

1.   Thomas Merton, *Thoughts in Solitude*, (New York: Farrar, Straus and Giroux, 1999), p. 79.

2.   N. Burton, P. Hart and J. Laughlin, eds., *The Asian Journal of Thomas Merton* (New York: New Directions, 1975), p. 308.

CHAPTER 7

1.   J. Krishnamurti, Ojai, Califronia, 6th Public Talk, 21 July 1955. Cited on the website: J Krishnamurti Online: http://www.jkrishnamurti.org/krishnamurti-teachings/view-daily-quote/20100615.php?t=Change. Accessed February 20, 2015.

CHAPTER 8

1.   Hazrat Inayat Kahn (1882-1927) of the Sufi International Order writes extensively about this and is worth reading. See *The Sufi Message of Hazrat Inayat Khan: Philosophy, Psychology and Mysticism* (ebook, Los Angeles: Library of Alexandria, 2000).

CHAPTER 9

1.   Mircea Eliade, *The Sacred and the Profane*, 63.

Sources

Andrews, Ted. *Animal Speak*. St. Paul, MN: Llewellyn Publications, 1993.

Bohm, David. *Wholeness and the Implicate Order*. London: Routledge, 1980.

Brahmdev, Swami. *Questions and Answers*. Uttaranchal, India: Aurovalley Ashram, 2006.

Buxton, Simon. *The Shamanic Way of the Bee*. Rochester, VT: Destiny Books, 2004.

Cowan, Tom. *Fire in the Head: Shamanism and the Celtic Spirit*. New York: HarperCollins Publisher, 1993.

Dychtwald, Ken. *BodyMind*. New York: Tarcher-Putnam, 1986.

Eckhart, Meister. *Selected Treatises and Sermons*. Translated by J. M. Clark and J. V. Skinner. London: Fount, 1994.

Eliade, Mircea. *Shamanism: Archaic Techniques of Ecstacy*. Princeton, NJ: Princeton University Press, 1964.

_____. *The Sacred and the Profane: The Nature of Religion*. New York: Harcourt, 1987.

Freke, Timothy, and Peter Gandy. *The Jesus Mysteries: Was the Original Jesus a Pagan God?* New York: Three Rivers Press, 1999.

Harner, Michael. *The Way of the Shaman*. New York: HarperCollins Publishers, 1990.

Harpur, Tom. *The Pagan Christ*. New York: Walker & Company, 2004.

James, William. *The Varieties of Religious Experience*. New York: Barnes & Noble Classics, 2004.

Jung, C. G. *Collected Works*. Vol. 14. *Mysterium Coniunctionis*. Princeton, NJ: Princeton University Press, 1989.

_____. *Psychology and Religion*. New York: Yale University Press, Inc., 1938.

MacLeod, Ainslee. *The Instruction*. Boulder, CO: Sounds True, Inc., 2007.

_____. *The Transformation*. Boulder, CO: Sounds True, Inc., 2010.

Monaghan, Patricia. *The New Book of Goddesses & Heroines*. Woodbury, MN: Llewellyn Publications, 1997.

Newell, John Philip. *A New Harmony: The Spirit, the Earth, and the Human Soul*. San Francisco, CA: Jossey-Bass, 2011.

Norton, Felicia, and Charles Smith. *An Emerald Earth: Cultivating a Natural Spirituality and Serving Beauty in Our World*. New York: TwoSeasJoin Press, 2008.

Perls, Frederick S. *Gestalt Therapy Verbatim*. Gouldboro, ME: The Gestalt Journal Press, 1992.

Plato. *Protagoras*. Translated by Benjamin Jowett. Rockville, MD: Serenity Publishers, 2009.

Prabhupada, A.C. Bhaktivedanta Swami. *Bhagavad-Gita As It Is*. Los Angeles, CA: Bhaktivedanta Book Trust International, Inc., 1989.

Pughe, Roberta, and Paula Anema Sohl. *Resurrecting Eve: Women of Faith Challenge the Fundamentalist Agenda*. Ashland, OR: White Cloud Press, 2007.

Redmond, Layne. *When the Drummers Were Women*. New York: Three Rivers Press, 1997.

Rumi, Jalal al-Din. *The Essential Rumi*. Translated by Coleman Barks. New York: Penguin Books, 1999.

Schweig, Graham M. *Bhagavad Gita: The Beloved Lord's Secret Love Song*. New York: HarperCollins Publishers, 2007.

Tolle, Eckhart. *The Power of Now: A Guide to Spiritual Enlightenment*. Novato, CA: New World Library, 1999.

_____. *New Earth: Awakening to Your Life's Purpose*. New York: Penguin Group Inc., 2005.

Van der Kolk, Bessel A. *Psychological Trauma*. Arlington, VA: American Psychiatric Publishing, 1987.

Varenne, Jean. *Yoga and the Hindu Tradition*. Translated by Derek Coleman. New Delhi: Motilal Barnarsidass, 1989.

Villoldo, Dr. Alberto. *Shaman, Healer, Sage: How to Heal Yourself & Others with the Energy Medicine of the Americas*. New York: Harmony Books, 2000.

Wesselman, Hank. *Medicinemaker: Mystic Encounters Along the Shaman's Path*. New York: Bantam Books, 1998.

Yeatts, Tabatha. *Albert Einstein*. New York: Sterling Publishing, 2007.

ABOUT THE AUTHOR

 ROBERTA PUGHE, MA, EDS, is a Gestalt psychotherapist (licensed marriage and family therapist) and contemporary shamanic practitioner who has had a private practice for over thirty years. Roberta's experience combines a solid foundation in systems therapy, gestalt theory, and theological studies. In addition to her clinical practice, Roberta is an educator, conference leader, and published author. Her book *Resurrecting Eve* (White Cloud Press) was released in 2007. Increasingly, she is bringing her deep knowledge of shamanism to bear on her therapeutic work with couples, individuals, and families, finding that integrating these ancient paths—in the face of our harried modern lives—offers access to deep healing, soul retrieval, and profound insights about the interconnectedness of all of life. Roberta's current passion is to foster embodied, soulful communities as "Domination-Free Orders," nurturing nonviolence, inclusivity, and social transformation for the global world, talking back with a new paradigm to the isolation, individualism, and alienation that dominate American culture. Her home and practice are located in Princeton, New Jersey.